C

1
Introducing
Corfu

Visitors and settlers have been delighted by the green and pleasant island of Corfu for thousands of years. It was already a popular holiday destination in Roman times, and today it is one of the busiest spots in the Mediterranean.

Corfu has a population of about 100,000 packed into its 593km² (229 sq miles), making it one of the most densely populated parts of Greece – and that's without the annual impact of almost one million visitors. Nevertheless, such figures are misleading, as over one-third of the population lives in the capital, Corfu Town. There is some 217km (135 miles) of glorious coastline for visitors to enjoy, and the vast majority of these shoehorn themselves into a handful of bustling seaside resorts, so escape from the crowds is still possible. And though few coastal villages are totally untouched by tourism, some have not yet been taken over by it.

What has made Corfu so popular? For one thing, it can boast some of the best **beaches** in Greece. Its climate is **warm** for most of the year and regular rainfall makes Corfu an unusually green Mediterranean island. The **scenery** is outstanding, with the north dominated by the majestic slopes of Mount Pandokrator, and the **people** possess the traditional Greek friendliness (in Greek the word for 'stranger' and 'guest' is the same). Inland are **hillside and mountain villages** where life goes on much as it must have done a hundred or even a thousand years ago. And finally, **Corfu Town** is probably the most attractive capital to be found in any of the Greek islands.

Opposite: *This peaceful scene at Pondikoníssi greets travellers arriving by air.*

THE LAND

The most northerly of the seven Ionian Islands, Corfu
measures just 58km (36 miles) lengthwise and 27km (17
miles) across at its widest point. From north to south it is
shaped like a handle or a sickle, a form reflected in past
names for the island in Greek. It can be roughly divided
into three main areas: the **mountainous north**, the **hilly
centre** and the more **low-lying south**. Much of the coast
is sandy or pebbly, giving beautiful long stretches of
beach, particularly to the west of the Andinióti Lagoon
on the north coast, and along Lake Korission in the
southwest. There are also lengthy expanses of **cliffs**,
especially on the west coast to the north of the holiday
resort of Ermónes. A series of unusual low cliffs
spectacularly striped with layers of clay and sand can be
seen at Sidhari and Perouládhes in the north.

North Corfu is dominated by the peak of **Mount
Pandokrator**, rising to 906m (2972ft) and sometimes
lightly capped with snow in winter. Corfu's wet, warm
climate ensures that the slopes are thickly carpeted with
a wide variety of flowers in the spring, notably many
species of orchid. From the mountain's summit to the
nearest beach resorts, such as Nissáki and Barbáti, is less
than 3km (2 miles), which gives some idea of how
steeply the slopes rise behind these beaches and the
spectacular setting provided by the mountain.

Right: *There are still far
more olive trees than
tourists on Corfu, but both
provide an annual income
for the Corfiots.*
Opposite: *The beach and
bay at Barbáti are typical of
the dramatic settings of
northern Corfu.*

Rivers and Lagoons

While Corfu is too small to have any really large flowing rivers, its regular rainfall means that it is much better watered than almost any other Greek island. There are several small rivers, the most notable being the **Rópa River**, which waters the fertile Rópa Plain in the centre of the island. It also waters Corfu's sole golf course, where its meandering course makes it a hazard at almost every hole. When not distracting golfers, the river irrigates the plain, where vines and cereals grow in abundance.

There are three large lagoons. The **Andinióti Lagoon** on the north coast is in a fairly undeveloped area – though there is one popular beach close by – which means that wildlife can flourish in its waters and surrounding reed beds. By contrast, the **Halikiopoulos Lagoon** to the immediate south of Corfu Town is now the site of the airport runway; despite that, it still serves as home to rare white egrets and families of otters. Egrets can also be found at **Lake Korission** in the south, along with ibis, avocets, orchids . . . and Greek hunters. Hunting is as popular on Corfu as on other Mediterranean islands.

BIRDLIFE

Corfu may not be the best spot in the Mediterranean for birdwatching, but for such a small island it offers a great deal of variety to the ornithologist. There are mountain slopes, cypress and olive groves, coastal cliffs and lagoons. The Halikiopoulos Lagoon, within walking distance of Corfu Town, is the winter home of the rare white egret as well as the Dalmatian pelican, and Audouin's gull also visits Corfu in winter. Both peregrine and Eleonora's falcons inhabit the cliffs, while olive warblers are, unsurprisingly, quite common. Look out, too, for the blue rock thrush.

Greece has some of the cleanest waters in the Mediterranean, with beaches safe for family bathing.

Climate

Corfu has a very appealing climate, which is why there are enclaves of people from northern Europe who have settled on the island. In midsummer the temperature will generally be around 31°C (88°F), and the whole island will be comfortably warm from April through to November – in May, the average temperature is about 20°C (68°F). In high summer you can expect 11 or 12 hours of sunshine a day, and even in December there is an average of three hours' sunshine per day. January and February are the coldest months, and there are very occasional frosts and snowfalls.

The island has **regular rainfall**, with the probability of a few showers even in July and August; in fact, Corfu is the wettest place in Greece, with almost as much rainfall as London. This does have its advantages. Corfu is green and fertile, with a wide variety of produce, a good wine-making industry and none of the water-shortage problems experienced by some of the Aegean islands towards the end of their bone-dry summers. July is the driest month, when just a few isolated showers are likely, falling on an average of two days. There is fairly regular rainfall from November through to March, and in October or November there will be a short period of thunderstorms, as the warmer weather finally breaks and gives way to winter.

IT'S AN ILL WIND . . .

As in most Mediterranean countries, there are periods when strong winds blow, but these are less regular and less predictable on Corfu than elsewhere. In winter cold winds can blow from the northeast and the south, but in the summer the wind is more likely to be a northwesterly. Some of the western coastal resorts are therefore particularly popular with windsurfers and other watersports enthusiasts. Winds are not generally so uncomfortable as to make any period worth avoiding, but it is notable that one of the great Corfiot defeats of would-be Turkish invaders was aided by strong winds and violent storms – and this took place in August 1716.

Wildlife

There is plenty of wild life in Corfu's nightclubs in August – but the island is not short of the natural history variety either. Indeed, it was the richness of its wildlife that enchanted the British zoologist Gerald Durrell, whose boyhood was spent on the island (see box, page 70).

There are rarities, but you need dedication and luck to see them. The seas around Corfu, are home to a few of Europe's remaining tiny population of **Mediterranean monk seals**. These animals were mentioned by Homer, but today only 400 survive. More common – but still endangered – is the **loggerhead turtle**; some can be found around Corfu though they tend to prefer the more southerly Ionian islands. Only the extremely lucky visitor will spot a **jackal**: very few of these wild dogs are left in Europe, but some still carry on their nocturnal lives on Corfu. You are far more likely to see hares, bats and hedgehogs.

Spring is the best time to visit, when the days are warm, the plants are burgeoning and the bird populations are increased by migrant species. There is a

THE HERB GARDEN

Corfu is as rich in herbs as it is in every other kind of plant, and local people can often be seen picking these in the hills, or even on unpromising looking sites in towns. To be effective, the herbs have to be gathered on the right Saint's Day. Oregano is picked on 24 June, the feast of St John, while basil must wait till 14 September, the feast of the Holy Cross. Other common herbs include camomile, thyme and sage, this last being made into a tea as well as being used widely in cooking.

In spring the island is bursting with colour, and visitors are few in number.

Mount Pandokrator is home to many beautiful flowers such as this Sternbergia Lutea, *known in Greek as the* Krinaki *or* Agriokrinos.

EUROPE'S MOST ENDANGERED MAMMAL

The **Mediterranean monk seal** has been around for 15 million years, but today it is Europe's most endangered mammal. Its relative, the Caribbean monk seal, became extinct in the 1950s. As its name suggests, it is a retiring creature, easily disturbed and easily affected by pollution. There are small numbers of monk seals living in the seas around Corfu. Should you see one you should make no attempt to approach, and if anyone offers you a trip to see seals, politely refuse, explaining why. You should also avoid leaving rubbish in the sea, or on the shore where it can be washed out to sea.

---

rich variety of habitat for the wildlife, from meadows and marshes to mountain slopes, lagoons, cliff faces and vast groves of olive and cypress trees. Even in Corfu Town, in the green retreat of the British Cemetery, you will find orchids on the ground and be able to watch for redstarts or goldcrests high in the trees.

Mount Pandokrator is the big attraction, and is dealt with in more detail elsewhere (page 72), but no naturalist should miss a climb to its summit or the chance to spend a few days exploring its slopes in search of **orchids** or **raptors**. Kestrels are common, but red-footed falcons, Egyptian vultures, buzzards, goshawks, peregrines and golden eagles also occur. In the olive groves which cover most of the island you will find several varieties of warbler, flycatcher or shrike, and at night you might hear the distinctive bell-like sound of the Scop's owl calling. Probably the most colourful spring visitor is the **bee-eater**, arriving from Africa and unmistakable when it flies into the air from its perch in an explosion of silky greens, blues and golds.

There are **tortoises** too, and several species of **snake** and **lizard**, as well as abundant **butterflies** attracted by the fragrant herbs and plants of Corfu's *maquis* vegetation. Most of the snakes are non-poisonous, and in any case they are very adept at getting out of the way when they feel the vibration of human footsteps. The only very venomous snake is the **sand viper**, but this is mainly nocturnal; it is distinctive, having what looks like a horn above each eye. Should you be unlucky enough to be bitten, you must seek medical attention. Most visitors to the island, however, suffer nothing worse than the occasional mosquito bite.

HISTORY IN BRIEF

Who were the first inhabitants of Corfu? Archaeological finds near Gardiki Castle in central Corfu have been dated as far back as 40,000BC, and a site near Sidhari on the northwest coast was probably a pre-Neolithic settlement in the 7th millennium BC. Several Bronze Age settlements from the 2nd millennium BC have been discovered, perhaps the real-life homes of the Phaeaceans encountered by Homer's Odysseus.

We have more detailed knowledge of events from the 8th century BC onwards. Settlers came from Illyria, on the eastern Adriatic coast, followed by people from Eretria on the Aegean island now called Évia (Euboea). Then came invasions by pirates from that same eastern Adriatic coast, notably from Dalmatia. But the first important colonisation was that of the **Corinthians** in about 734BC, which brought a measure of stability to the island until the Corfiots started initiating their own policies without recourse to their overlords from the city-state of Corinth. The Corinthians tried to reassert their authority, but this only led to a struggle for power culminating in a sea battle in 644BC, the earliest recorded in Greek waters, which the Corfiots won.

The Corfiots and Corinthians subsequently became allies, but not for long, and the rivalry between them was

> **THE ODYSSEY**
>
> Homer's epic poem is frequently cited as the first novel because of its strong narrative and use of flashbacks. It tells the story of Odysseus, who, after fighting in the Trojan War, is making his way back to his native island of Ithaca and his wife Penelope and son Telemachus. It is, to put it mildly, an eventful journey. Odysseus encounters one-eyed giants, sirens, whirlpools, the lotus-eaters and angry gods, and even descends into the Underworld. Corfu is generally accepted as the likely setting for the fictional island of Scheria, where Odysseus is washed ashore after shipwreck and where he recounts most of his tale.

Old storage pots would once have been filled with grain or oil.

THE BIRTH OF DEMOCRACY

In about the 9th century BC a new type of political entity made its appearance in the ancient world: the **city-state** or *polis* (as in 'metropolis'). Wherever the Greeks settled they formed city-states, each with its own code of laws. This was the beginning of democracy, as city-states were run by the citizens rather than by hereditary rulers (though not everyone qualified as a 'citizen'). By the 5th century BC the two most powerful city-states were Athens and Sparta. In the bloody Peloponnesian War Corfu allied with the ultimately victorious Athens.

to be one of the major causes of the Peloponnesian War. The Corfiots had founded several colonies on the mainland, among them one at Epidamnus. When a civil war here forced out the rulers, Corfu refused to support the victorious democrats, who turned to Corinth for help. The Corinthians sent troops to Epidamnus, angering the Corfiots who sent a fleet and defeated the Corinthians at sea. The Corinthians regrouped with additional forces, and the Corfiots turned to Corinth's great rival, Athens, for help. The Athenians supported them, and together they defeated the Corinthian warships.

It was the Corinthians' anger against Athens for this act that helped fuel the **Peloponnesian War** (431–404BC). Initially the Corfiots supported the Athenians, but later they had to turn their attention to their home island where civil war was breaking out. The losses in the war on the Peloponnese, and subsequently on Corfu itself, caused a decline in the island's power, leading to an invasion of Corfu by the armies of Sparta in 375BC. However, the Athenians soon came to the help of their old allies, driving the Spartans from the island.

The Roman Empire

Corfu's independence did not last long. Another invasion by the Illyrians caused them to turn to Rome for help in 229BC, and for almost 600 years Corfu was part of the Roman Empire, followed by another 930 years of Byzantine rule after the division of the Roman Empire. Among the more notable events during the early period of Roman rule was the **arrival of Christianity** on Corfu in the 1st century AD, brought by St Jason and St Sosipater. An 11th-century church dedicated to them can be found in the southern suburbs of Corfu Town, just before you reach the Mon Repos estate. The first Christian church was built by these disciples of St. Paul on the islet of Pythia, and dedicated to Ayios Stefanos. The death of Constantine the Great in 337AD brought about the partition of the Roman state with Corfu becoming a part of the eastern division until 455AD.

TROUBLESOME NEIGHBOURS

Illyria was an area on the eastern and northeastern coasts of the Adriatic, to the east of modern Italy. Greece established colonies here in the 7th and 6th centuries BC. The Illyrians waged war wherever they went, but the region was finally conquered by Rome in the 1st century BC, and eventually became part of the Byzantine Empire after the fall of Rome.

This chapel is built into the rock of the Byzantine castle of Angelókastro.

Byzantine Rule

The Byzantine period was a far from peaceful one for the island. **Vandals** sacked Corfu in 455, and out of frustration at not being able to capture the capital they wreaked great havoc on much of the rest of the island. Later, Corfu was caught up in the battles between the Roman forces and the **Goths**; after overrunning Italy, the Goths sacked Corfu in 562 and made it a base from which they could attack parts of the Greek mainland.

In the 11th century, when the **Norman forces** were pushing south, they in their turn sought to seize Corfu as a base, to enable them to extend their territory eastwards into the Balkans. The main attack was initially made by the son of the Norman military leader, **Robert Guiscard**, but Guiscard himself was obliged to enter the fray and helped take the island. He faced a later rebellion when both Byzantine and Venetian ships rallied to the Corfiot cause, but the powerful Norman armies were victorious. The Norman forces were finally vanquished in 1147, again by a joint effort of Corfiot, Byzantine and Venetian troops but other changes were soon to come.

> **NORMAN CONQUEROR**
>
> Robert Guiscard was born in Normandy in the early part of the 11th century, and went to Italy where he eventually became leader of the Normans there. He became an ally of Pope Nicholas II, and went on to capture large parts of the Balkans. He died of fever on Kefallonia in 1085, when he was about 70 years old and still fighting.

When the Byzantine Empire was finally defeated by the Crusaders in 1204, Corfu was put under Venetian rule, but in 1214 the island was invaded yet again, this time by the forces of the Despot of Epirus, **Michael Angelos Komnenos II**. The remains of the fortress of Angelókastro which he built near Paleokastrítsa can still be seen. When the Despot was later threatened by the powerful Sicilian king, Manfred, he gave Manfred the hand of his daughter, together with Corfu, as part of the dowry. In 1267 the Pope gave the island to Charles of Anjou, who was also King of Naples, in recognition of his support for the Papacy against the Holy Roman Empire, and it remained under Angevin control for over a hundred years, when the Orthodox church was increasingly repressed.

Venetian Rule (1386–1797)

In 1386 a group of leading Corfiots, anxious for stability after a period of disputed claims to the island, approached the Doge of Venice for protection. The Venetian forces took Corfu by storm, and in 1402 Venice officially claimed it, paying the King of Naples 30,000 gold ducats in compensation. The ensuing four centuries of rule from Venice had many effects, but two in particular stand out.

Firstly, Corfu was the only part of modern Greece never to fall to **the Turks**, despite vigorous Turkish attempts to occupy it. The Venetians made the island their main arsenal in Greece and built many fortifications, all of which helped the islanders to repel repeated Turkish attacks during the 15th to 18th centuries. These brought intense suffering to the Corfiot population, but the Old Fortress in Corfu Town never

---

DEATH AND DEFIANCE

In 1537, the infamous pirate-admiral Barbarossa, under the rule of Suleiman the Magnificent, invaded Corfu. He slaughtered the unfortunate inhabitants who had been cruelly locked outside Corfu Town's Old Fortress and burned the entire island before being driven off, taking with him 20,000 Corfiot slaves for sale in Constantinople. Just 34 years later, Sinan Pasha – another thug in the mould of Barbarossa – renewed the Turkish assault and, after three attacks, had literally decimated the island's population. But he failed to take the Old Fortress. In 1716 the Turks returned. After a six-week struggle, when the defenders were apparently about to succumb, the enemy miraculously retreated, due – so the islanders would maintain – to the intervention of St Spiridhon, their patron saint, who raised a violent storm.

succumbed. Given the antagonism that still exists today between the Greeks and the Turks, the Corfiots are proud to be able to claim that their island never fell.

A second, much more important and permanent monument to the influence of the Venetians is visible wherever you look on Corfu: **the olive tree**. Although the Venetians did not introduce the tree to the island – they are believed to have grown here for at least 5000 years – they encouraged the farmers to grow them as intensively as possible to meet the tremendous demand for olive oil back in Venice. Other native species were uprooted as the Venetians forced the islanders to cultivate olive trees, which adapted happily to the soil and climate and flourished throughout the island, to the extent that today they occupy about 30% of the land.

OLIVE CULTURE

Corfiots have been cultivating the olive for 5000 years, and there are said to be somewhere between three and four million olive trees on Corfu today. Harvesting is carried out in a most unusual way. The Corfiot growers do not pick the fruit or beat the branches with sticks, as is done elsewhere, but let the olives fall to the ground naturally. Neither do they prune their trees, with the result that they have some of the largest trees in Greece. It is quite usual in Greece for an olive tree to be owned by someone other than the owner of the land on which it grows, but the landowner must allow access to the tree.

The Venetians had a great impact on the look of the **buildings** as well as the countryside. Their influence can be seen everywhere in Corfu Town, with its many tall, balconied buildings, the shutters painted an Italian green rather than the usual bright blue of the Greek Aegean islands. Most churches, too, are in Venetian style, with separate bell towers and red-tiled roofs. The Venetians fortified the island, building Corfu Town's Old Fortress in 1550, followed by the New Fortress a mere 30 or so years later; gun batteries were everywhere.

Of less importance to Venice were the Corfiot working people. As long as they continued to produce the required olive oil, their education, emancipation and good health could be ignored. During the 17th century the arts flourished in the capital, while the people working the land suffered **plague and poverty**. In 1610 the Corfiot villagers had refused to pay rent to the landowners, forming armed vigilante bands to prevent Venetian troops from entering their villages to enforce the law. The dispute was settled diplomatically, but there were three more revolts in the 1640s and 1650s, accompanied by much violence, as the Venetian army attempted to put down the rebellions. Meanwhile, the aristocracy on Corfu had published its *Libro d'Oro* ('Golden Book'), which listed the most noble families, as did a similar book in Venice itself: Corfu and the Venetian empire were both in decline and the French in ascendancy.

The Listón, designed by Frenchman, Mathieu de Lesseps, was built in 1807.

The French in Corfu

Napoleon Bonaparte's General Gentili captured Corfu in 1797, and the French forces were greeted as liberators. They burned the 'Golden Book' in the main square and planted a Tree of Liberty on the site of the fire. With memories of the French Revolution (1789) still fresh in their minds, the Corfiots were delighted to have overthrown the Venetian ruling class.

Less delighted at the prospect of French rule in the Ionian Islands were the other great powers – Britain, Russia and, in particular, Turkey. In 1799 a joint Russian-Turkish venture took the island back from the French and declared the Ionian Islands a **'Septinsular Republic'**, the first glimmerings of the eventual emergence of a separate Greek state – another source of great Corfiot pride. The republic proved short-lived, as Russia and Turkey were soon at war with each other, and in 1807 the French returned to Corfu for a brief but productive period of seven years. During this time, the Ionian Academy was founded and use of the Greek language was re-established to replace Italian; printing was introduced, as too were the potato and the tomato, important additions to the island's agriculture.

British Rule (1814–1864)

When Napoleon abdicated in 1814, both Britain and Austria claimed Corfu. In 1815 a treaty was signed which declared that, while the Ionian Islands would form a free and independent state, they would come under the exclusive protection of Britain. This was another short but vital period in the development of the Ionian Islands, as both they and Greece moved towards total independence and ultimate unification.

> ### THE BRITISH INHERITANCE
>
> In addition to cricket, Corfu has retained a taste, unique in Greece, for several other British traditions. A fondness for Christmas pudding is one of them, no doubt aided by the sizable British community living on Corfu and largely catering for the tourist trade. Ginger beer (*tsitsi bira*) was another peculiarity, though hard to find these days, while brass bands are still popular. The strains of a trombone or trumpet being practised can frequently be heard wafting from windows in the town centre, while the bands can be seen marching at any of the island's major religious processions.

The British Garrison Church of St George was built in typical Greek style, though it is far from typical of Corfiot architecture.

Corfu's mainland neighbour, the region of Epirus, has had its share of despotic rulers. However, the Despot of Epirus was welcomed by the Corfiots in 1214 when he took the island from the Venetians. The ensuing rule of the Despotate was a golden period, when Orthodox Christianity flourished and Corfu prospered. A less benign figure is that of Ali Pasha, the maverick Turkish provincial governor of Epirus who, in defiance of the Ottoman central authority, carved out his own Greek empire in the early years of the 19th century. He was supported by the first British High Commissioner of Corfu, Sir Thomas Maitland, who in 1817 ceded him the mainland port of Parga – whose inhabitants promptly emigrated to Corfu. Ali Pasha's activities, in distracting the Ottomans, facilitated the Greek uprising of 1821.

Greek now became Corfu's official language and the Ionian Academy its first University. The road network was improved and an aqueduct built to bring fresh water to Corfu Town. The face of the capital changed, with many new buildings and monuments going up; most still stand today and, as for instance the Palace of St Michael and St George and the Maitland Rotunda, add to the elegance of the town.

Meanwhile, momentum was gathering in the movement towards unification with Greece, which in 1829 had formally gained its **independence** from the Ottoman Empire after four centuries of Turkish rule. Britain wanted to hold on to Corfu because of its useful position between the ports of Italy and those of the Eastern Mediterranean, but the Corfiot determination to be part of the new Greek state won out, and the last British Commissioner, Sir Henry Storks, was appointed in 1859. Five years later, on 21 May 1864, the British flag was replaced by the Greek flag, flying for the first time above the Old Fortress in Corfu Town.

One of Corfu's most prominent sons, **Ioannis Kapodistrias**, became the first President of modern Greece after his close involvement in the struggle for liberation; sadly he did not live to see Corfu's independence as he was assassinated in 1831. Another important Corfiot statesman was **George Theotokis**, who served as Greece's prime minister several times.

Modern Corfu

Corfu grew increasingly attractive to visitors from both the Greek mainland and abroad, and in the late 19th and early 20th centuries was becoming a fashionable and prosperous island. The Mon Repos estate and villa served as the summer residence for the Greek royal family, while Elizabeth of Austria was such a regular visitor to the island that she built her own palace, the Achillíon (now open to visitors and serving as a casino in the evenings – see page 105). After the assassination of Elizabeth, the Achillíon was eventually bought by the German Kaiser, Wilhelm II. You can see his 'throne', a favourite sunset-viewing spot near Pélekas, and his 'bridge', more of a jetty, built to provide him with easy access to the Achillíon when he arrived by sea.

Corfu was officially neutral during World War I, although it was used as a naval base (see box). It was in 1923 that the island entered the world stage when it came under attack from the Italians in what became known as the Corfu Incident. Arguments over Greece's northern border with Albania – continuing to this day – were being thrashed out by a commission, when the Italian delegate was murdered. His killer was never discovered. Because this happened on Greek soil, Mussolini attacked Corfu, Greece's nearest point to Italy, and occupied the island. Through the intervention of the League of Nations the Italians were eventually persuaded to leave.

Italy reoccupied Corfu during World War II, followed by the Germans; the island was liberated in 1944 by the advancing Allied Army. Since then, there has been a long period of stability, with a steady increase in tourism bringing prosperity to the islanders.

SERBIAN TRAGEDY

During World War I Corfu declared its neutrality, but was seized for use as a naval base by the British, French and Italian allies in December 1915. After the defeat of Serbia by Austria in 1916, the Serbian government and its troops retreated to Corfu. Already ravaged by cholera, many more of the Serbians died there from injuries, further disease and overcrowded living conditions. Their graves can be found in a Serbian cemetery on Vidos Island.

Left: *The Achillíon Palace has been a royal home, hospital and film set, and is now both a museum and a casino.*
Opposite: *Ioannis Kapodistrias became modern Greece's first President in 1827; his statue now stands at the top of the street which bears his name, Kapodistriou.*

FLYING THE FLAG

The motto of those who fought for Greek independence against the Turks was *ELEUTHERÍA I THÁNATOS* (FREEDOM OR DEATH), and the nine stripes of the national flag are said to represent those nine syllables. The general design had been around since the independence declaration on 13 January 1822, though the flag was not officially adopted until 1833 when Otto of Bavaria became the first king of the independent Greek state. Fortuitously, the blue and white colours, which had been the traditional Greek colours since at least the wars with the Turks, were also Otto's family colours. The design has gone through a number of variations and shades of blue over the years, but the flag one sees today has nine stripes in the original pale blue and white with, in the top left corner, a cross against a white background.

Greece in the 20th century

Although Corfu itself has enjoyed a period of relative stability since unification with Greece, the country as a whole has had a turbulent 20th century. An ignominious end to World War I saw Greece defeated in its attempts to continue hostilities and capture Turkey, and in 1923 there was an **exchange of religious populations** when 388,000 Muslim Turks left Greece and no less than 1,300,000 Christian Greeks came home from Turkey. This had a shattering effect on a poor country whose population at that time was less than five million.

After German occupation of the mainland during World War II, liberation only plunged the country into a vicious **Civil War** which lasted until late 1949. In 1967 there was further turmoil when a group led by Army Colonels seized power from an increasingly left-wing government in a **military coup**. The Junta was to last for seven years, its downfall brought about by inept handling of the situation in Cyprus, which resulted in the Turkish invasion of the northern part of that island and a dispute which, 20 years later, is still unresolved.

In the first post-Junta democratic elections of November 1974, the New Democracy Party came to power, and shortly afterwards a referendum voted for the **abolition of the monarchy**. King Constantine – who had gone into exile after his support of the Colonels' Junta – was replaced by a president. The royal summer residence on Corfu, Mon Repos, has been in limbo ever since, though it may soon be opened to the public.

Several new political parties were formed in the wake of the Colonels, among them the socialist PASOK party, which was voted into power in the 1981 general elections. They formed the Greek government until 1989, but lost overall control after revelations of financial scandals involving the embezzlement of some £120 million from the Bank of Crete by one of its directors; PASOK ministers, and possibly even Prime Minister Papandreou, were implicated.

A series of unresolved elections followed, until in April 1990 the right-wing New Democracy Party was

HISTORICAL CALENDAR

40,000BC Evidence of Palaeolithic people
7000BC Earliest known settlements.
734BC Colonised by Corinthians.
644BC Corfu victorious over Corinthians in sea battle.
431BC The Peloponnesian War begins in Greece. Corfu declares war on Corinth.
375BC Corfu invaded by Spartan armies.

229BC Corfu becomes part of Roman Empire.
AD455 Vandals sack Corfu.
562 Goths sack Corfu.
1020 Pisa annexes Corfu.
1082 Robert Guiscard defeats the Byzantine forces and occupies Corfu.
1147 Normans forced out.
1214 Invasion by Despot of Epirus.
1267–1386 Rule by King of Naples.

1386–1797 Venetian rule.
1797 French capture Corfu.
1814–64 The British Protectorate.
1864 Corfu gains independence and becomes a part of modern Greece.
1923 The Corfu Incident; island invaded by Italian forces.
1941–4 Occupation by Axis forces during World War II.
1994 Corfu democratically elects Prefect for first time.

elected with a single-seat majority. The new government's austerity measures proved unpopular, and in 1993 the PASOK party was returned to government with 47% of the vote against New Democracy's 39%. Mr Papandreou was back in power despite past scandals, his poor health, his age (74) and his 1988 affair with the air hostess who later became his wife.

The Greek Parliament building on Athens' Syntagma Square from where Corfu is governed.

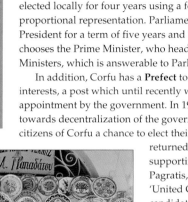

IN WINTER

Any Greek island is a very different place in winter. Not only do the visitors go home but so too do many Greeks, who return to businesses in America, Australia or Athens. It can be a good time to visit Corfu Town, as the town remains lively, museums remain open, prices are lower, people have more time for you, and there can be many mild, sunny days.

GOVERNMENT AND ECONOMY

Corfu is governed from Athens as a part of Greece. The **Greek parliament**, or *Voulí*, is made up of 300 members elected locally for four years using a form of proportional representation. Parliament elects a President for a term of five years and he in his turn chooses the Prime Minister, who heads the Council of Ministers, which is answerable to Parliament.

In addition, Corfu has a **Prefect** to represent its interests, a post which until recently was a political appointment by the government. In 1994 a move towards decentralization of the government gave the citizens of Corfu a chance to elect their own Prefect. They

returned the PASOK-supporting Andreas Pagratis, who stood as a 'United Corfiot Movement' candidate and received over 32,000 votes – the support of 52% of the electorate.

The various regions of Corfu also have their own local, democratically elected politicians, headed by a **mayor**. Since 1990 the Mayor of the Municipality of Corfu has been Chrysanthos Sarlis, returned in 1994 with 58% of the vote. Nominally a PASOK candidate, he owes his undoubted popularity to a general disregard for extreme party politics, and a preference for working with both left and right to pursue the best interests of Corfu Town and the surrounding areas.

Economy

About eight million tourists visit Greece every year,
bringing an estimated two billion dollars into the
economy. Corfu gets about 900,000 of these visitors,
worth up to 250 million dollars to the island's economy.
About one-third of the working population is employed
in **tourism** or ancillary service industries, such as
construction, food and drink processing plants and the
making of leather and other goods predominantly sold
as souvenirs. Yet despite the dramatic increase in the
importance of the tourist industry since the 1950s, Corfu
is still very largely an **agricultural island**: 60% of its
population works on the land, and 60% of the island is
cultivated. Half of the cultivated land is given over to
olive trees, an estimated 3.5 million of them. Evidence of
fishing may be widely apparent – boats bobbing on the
sea or fishermen sitting mending their nets in the coastal
villages – but fishing is now more a tradition than an
industry.

After olive trees and tourists, Corfu is notable for its
healthy **wine industry**. Many island specialities are not
available elsewhere in Greece, so visitors should take the
chance to sample these. Greek wine will never compete
with the best of the rest of Europe, but there are some
very palatable table wines available. Corfu's kumquat
liqueur is unique to the island. Other **fruits** – oranges,
lemons, pears, peaches, apricots, apples, cherries and

melons – are grown, while
one of the delights of
walking on the island is the
opportunity to pick wild figs,
straight from the branch.
Also harvested are the nuts
from the carob tree, as well
as almonds and walnuts. The
principal **vegetables** to find
their way on to the
restaurant plate are potatoes,
tomatoes, cucumbers, beans,
onions and aubergines.

Opposite: *Tourism is
modern Greece's second
largest money-earner.*
Below: *Corfu is well
watered, and many rural
families keep at least a few
animals.*

GREEK ALPHABET

The Greek alphabet may look daunting at first, but it only takes an hour or so to memorize it. A knowledge of the alphabet will enable you to read road and other signs, and the destinations of local buses. The chart below shows upper and lower case characters of the alphabet, together with a guide to the pronunciation of their Greek names.

A	α	**ahl**fah
B	β	**vee**tah
Γ	γ	**ghah**mah
Δ	δ	**dhehl**tah
E	ε	**eh**pseelonn
Z	ζ	**zee**tah
H	η	**ee**tah
Θ	θ	**thee**tah
I	ι	**yeeo**tah
K	κ	**kah**pah
Λ	λ	**lahm**dhah
M	μ	mee
N	ν	nee
Ξ	ξ	ksee
O	ο	**o**meekron
Π	π	pee
P	ρ	ro
Σ	σ	**seegh**mah
T	τ	tahf
Y	υ	**ee**pseelonn
Φ	φ	fee
X	χ	khee
Ψ	ψ	psee
Ω	ω	om**eh**ghah

THE PEOPLE

Although Corfu and the other Ionian islands have been a part of Greece for less than 150 years, it is hard to imagine the Corfiot people being anything other than Greek. Of course there are the idiosyncratic British legacies of cricket, ginger beer and even Christmas pudding, but the Corfiot heart belongs to Greece. The language, the cooking and, most of all, the religion are Greek through and through.

Language

The official language is Greek, but in the tourist areas and capital you will find many speakers of English and other European languages, mainly German and Italian. Most information that the visitor is likely to need, such as on menus or notices and in museums, will be in both Greek and English, but this is not the case in the more rural areas. Similarly, while major road signs are in Greek and English, should you venture on to the minor roads – or wish to travel by bus round the island – it is useful to have a knowledge of the Greek alphabet.

Hand-made needle-lace is made all over Greece and is a popular souvenir. The lace is made by local women, often sitting on their doorsteps, chatting to fellow lacemakers and displaying their skills.

Religion

As in other parts of Greece, the population of Corfu is almost 100% **Greek Orthodox**. There is a small **Catholic** community, whose services are held in the Roman Catholic Cathedral in the Town Hall Square in Corfu Town, while the British left behind a tiny **Anglican** congregation, who worship in the church of the Holy Trinity on Mavili. There is also a very small **Jewish** population. Before World War II there were 4,000 Jews on Corfu, all of whom were removed by the Germans; only 80 returned.

The Greek Orthodox church plays a central role in Corfiot lives. The closeness of the church to everyday family life is evident in the role of the priest, a familiar figure seen not just in and around the church but in the streets, in the shops and sitting in the cafés, talking with the men of his flock over a cup of coffee. While treated with great respect, a priest is a man like other men to the Greeks. Ordinary priests may marry, although marriage prevents a priest rising beyond a certain level in the Orthodox church.

Greek Orthodox church services are informal affairs – almost as much social as religious occasions. Because they are long (up to three hours), worshippers may attend for a short while, wander away and perhaps return later on. Foreign visitors (suitably attired) are welcome to enter the church during a service. At any one time during a normal weekly service, the congregation might appear quite small, centered on a hard core of ubiquitous old ladies dressed in black, but on major feasts such as Easter or the festival of St Spiridhon (Corfu's patron saint), it becomes apparent just how many of the population still follow the faith.

One of the resident monks outside the chapel of the monastery in Paleokastrítsa.

WORRY BEADS

In a traditional Corfiot café, where the men gather to discuss everything from politics to the price of fish, you will see many of them playing with a small set of beads in one hand. These are known as worry beads, though the name seems rather a contradiction in a nation whose national slogan ought to be 'no problem'. In fact the beads are used more out of habit, while relaxing, than as a means of relieving tension. They are popular souvenirs, being typically Greek, and are available in all sizes, all materials and all colours in most souvenir shops. The Greek word for them is *Komboloi*.

Right: *Religious festivals play a big part in Corfu life, and visitors should never miss an opportunity to witness one of these events.*

Opposite: *More than 1600 years after his death, the remains of St Spiridhon are still intact and enshrined in the church dedicated to him.*

Festivals

Saints' days, Carnival and, above all, Easter are reasons for Corfiots to come out on the streets of towns and villages to celebrate. If your visit to a particular village coincides with the local saint's day, you can hardly fail to be caught up in the general atmosphere of excitement as the saint's image is taken from his church and paraded through the streets in a lively procession. Afterwards there will be feasting and dancing, which you may well be invited to join.

Easter

Most impressive of all is Easter, the principal festival of the Orthodox year. Corfu has its own spectacular way of observing the feast, making this a good time to visit Corfu Town, though the weather can be uncertain and the evenings will be cool. Solemn processions take place on Good Friday, a sombre day of mourning. Then on Easter Saturday morning St Spiridhon is carried through the streets in a brilliant procession. What follows is unique to Corfu Town. At 11:00 the streets are emptied and mayhem breaks out, as unwanted crockery is hurled from every window on to the streets below. Nobody knows the origin of this extraordinary custom.

PRIVATE TOURIST GUIDES

In Greece there are comparatively few official guides for hire through tourist offices, but in Corfu there is a Tourist Guide Association whose members speak most European languages and can be hired privately. Some notice may be needed in summer. The Association is based at Irini Dendrinou 1, Corfu Town, tel 0661-37847.

Evening mass climaxes at midnight, when the priest announces that Christ is risen. Electric lights are switched off and the priest ignites a solitary candle, from which the worshippers then light their own candles. Immediately church bells ring out, and fireworks blaze as the people make their way home for the Easter feast. In Corfu Town, the announcement of Christ's Resurrection is made from the bandstand on the Esplanade and is followed by church bells, music from the town bands and fireworks. Easter Sunday is a day for family celebrations, centred on a meal of roast lamb. There is often a communal evening celebration, at which visitors are welcome.

Other Festivals

Carnival is celebrated in Corfu Town on the last Sunday before Lent. After a colourful procession of floats accompanied by the town bands, an effigy representing the spirit of Carnival is ritually burnt.

'Clean Monday', the first day of Lent, is celebrated with a picnic (weather permitting) of seafood, salad, olives, special unleavened bread and *chalva*, a honeyed sweet.

Corfu's patron saint, **St Spiridhon**, is the focus of several festivals. His remains are paraded in four annual processions (see box on page 39) and his name day, 12 December, is shared by about half the male population of the island. On this day, the saint's body in its silver coffin is stood upright for the faithful to kiss his velvet slipper.

NAME DAYS

The Greeks celebrate not their birthday but their name day – the feast day of the saint after which they are named. So, every Maria or every Mikalis in one area will get together to celebrate in some way. This frequently means a big party. If you happen upon such an event, you will be made very welcome, although a small charge may be made to cover the cost of food and drink. Dancing and music frequently follow the meal.

SEAFOOD

Seafood can hardly be fresher than caught and served on the same day, but frozen fish is also served up and labelled as fresh in some tourist tavernas, so don't always believe what you're told. But if it's really fresh, the fish will be delicious. It will probably be expensive too, as fish stocks are low and prices high. Fish is priced by weight, so choose which piece you want rather than leaving it to the waiter – otherwise you could find yourself with an unexpectedly steep bill at the end of the meal.

Food and Drink

Corfiot cuisine is, for the most part, identical to that available anywhere else in Greece, but it does have two specialities which appear on almost every restaurant menu. *Sofríto* is a veal casserole served with a white sauce of garlic, onion, pepper, wine vinegar and anything else the chef puts in to produce his version of the dish. Some serve a beef *sofríto*, though strictly speaking it is a veal dish. So too is *pastitsáda*, another island speciality – veal served in a tomato sauce with pasta. However, the veal might be beef, the pasta might be any kind and the sauce depends on the whim of the chef, so try it in different restaurants. Less common, but well worth eating if you come across it, is *bourdéto*, a casserole of white fish, onions, olive oil and spicy red peppers.

Another feature of dining on Corfu is its **international flavour**. The vast numbers of tourists have created a range of restaurants to cater for them, including Italian, Chinese, British, French and Indian. Most of the chefs are Greek or British, and as adept at producing a chicken vindaloo as a plate of roast beef and Yorkshire pudding.

There are several types of Greek eating establishment. Best known is the **taverna**, a casual place where it is usual for the diner to wander into the kitchen to see what's cooking, rather than to order from the menu: not all the menu's dishes are necessarily available,

Stuffed peppers are popular and tasty, but best eaten at lunchtime when they are hot. Food is generally eaten lukewarm in the evenings.

while the kitchen might conceal some daily specials. Another feature is the paper or plastic tablecloths which are changed after each meal, and the little tumblers which serve as wine glasses. If all the tables are occupied when you arrive, simply wait: another table will probably be produced from somewhere and set out for you. Greek tavernas are surprisingly expandable.

A **restaurant** (*estiatório*) is more up-market: you should find a proper wineglass on the table, a linen tablecloth – and a surprised expression if you try to wander into the kitchen. Restaurants are more likely to take bookings, whereas at a taverna you generally turn up and take pot luck. For that reason, not all the recommended eating places in this guide have telephone numbers listed. Those with numbers take bookings, the others don't. In addition to regular tavernas and restaurants, there are places serving only fish (*psária*), and grill bars (*psistariés*), where

Greek wine wins no prizes, but aperitifs, spirits and liqueurs are plentiful and good value, with kumquat liqueur unique to Corfu.

the menu is generally limited to freshly grilled meats – chops or kebabs – and sometimes fish.

Greece is not noted for its **puddings**. A restaurant may have a small dessert menu, but in a taverna the only choice is likely to be fresh fruit (usually watermelon) or ice cream. It is common practice to eat your final course elsewhere, at a café which serves coffee, brandy and sticky Greek sweets such as *baklavá*.

The Greeks, generally, are not great drinkers and are likely to accompany a meal with no more than a can of beer or a soft drink. The pre-dinner favourite drink is **oúzo**, an aniseed-based drink similar to Pernod, which is served with a tumbler of water. You can drink the oúzo neat, taking an occasional sip of water, or you can dilute it by pouring water into the glass, which turns the oúzo milky. No Greek male would ever dilute his oúzo.

The cheapest wine available is **retsina**, an acquired taste – which many visitors never acquire. The white wine is flavoured with resin, originally from the wooden casks in which it was stored, but today the flavour is more likely to be added artificially. Not only is retsina cheap and available everywhere, it is in fact a good accompaniment to the oil-rich Greek food. Many tavernas serve it from the barrel, and a request for house wine will produce a metal jug of retsina. In it you have the authentic taste of Greece.

2
Corfu Town

Corfu Town (Kerkira to the locals) is as charming a capital as any in the Greek islands. With a population of about 30,000 it is small enough to have retained its human scale, yet large enough to be cosmopolitan. This international feel is due partly to of its location – it is closer to Italy than to Athens – and partly to its multicultural history.

The British presence may have lasted only 50 years, but it left a legacy unique in Greece, the game of cricket being just one eccentric part of this. On the grand scale, the villa of **Mon Repos** and the **Palace of St Michael and St George** were both built by the British. But the overall architectural appeal of the town is largely due to the Venetian influence, from the **Old and New Fortresses**, solid defences against onslaught from the sea, to the shuttered windows and narrow alleys. It was the French who first planted trees around the **Esplanade**, the grassy park at the heart of Corfu Town, and who were responsible for the **Listón**, the elegant terrace of cafés that borders the Esplanade, with its nod towards the Rue de Rivoli in Paris.

For all this, Corfu Town is undeniably Greek. Visit the Orthodox Cathedral or the church of the island's patron saint, St Spiridhon; explore the **Byzantine and Archaeological Museums**; eat in the tavernas, drink in the cafés of the Listón, visit the market near the New Fortress or watch the sun go down over the islets of **Vlachérna** and **Pondikoníssi** (Mouse Island), and you could be nowhere else in the world but Greece.

DON'T MISS

*** A visit to Kanóni and Mouse Island
*** Sitting in the Listón with a coffee
*** A stroll round the Old Town's narrow streets
*** The Museum of Asiatic Art's unique collection
** Paper Money Museum, unexpectedly fascinating
** Andivouniótissa Museum of Byzantine artefacts
** Church of St Spirídhon
** The Old Fortress with stunning views
** The imposing Gorgon Frieze in the Archaeological Museum.

Opposite: *The Listón, a touch of Parisian chic.*

Old and New Ports *

Corfu Town has two ports, both on the northern side of town. The **New Port**, in the suburb of Mandoúki, is used mainly for international ferry routes, along with some boats to other Greek islands and the mainland. From here it is a walkable distance into the town centre (unless your luggage is particularly heavy), or you can take a taxi from the rank outside; there is no bus service.

The smaller daily ferries to Igoumenítsa on the mainland and to the island of Paxos depart from the **Old Port**,

to the east of the New Fortress. Tickets for trips can be bought from any of the several ticket offices both behind and to the east of the port itself, on Athinagora and Donzelot streets. The Old Port is a low-key affair: as small fishing boats moored in the harbour rock gently on the water, you can imagine what Corfu Town might have been like in the old days, before the island became a magnet for tourism.

New Fortress *

The New Fortress, or Néo Froúrio ('new' because it was built some 30 years after the Old Fortress) dominates the Old Port. The Venetians started building it in 1576, and completed it 13 years later; the British added the buildings at the very top in 1815. The **view** from here – of Corfu Town, surrounding villages, Mount Pandokrator to the north and across to mainland Greece and Albania – is said to be splendid, but visitors are unable to confirm this for themselves: the Fortress is used as a training establishment by the Greek Navy and access is closed off.

However, some 70 million drachmas having been spent on providing facilities in the Fortress for the 1994 European Union summit conference, it is hoped that in the future the facilities will be available for other conferences, with perhaps the addition of an open-air theatre on the top. What visitors can already see down below is the lively fruit and vegetable **market** held daily in what was the moat. This can be reached through a small tunnel lying above and behind New Fortress Square. In the square itself is the small NTOG (National Tourist Office of Greece) Information Office, which has a few booklets relating to Corfu and hundreds covering the rest of Greece.

The Old Port has domestic ferries and other craft; international services depart from the New Port.

Old Town ★★★

The well used phrase 'a maze of streets' takes on fresh significance when you start to meander through the **narrow streets** and even narrower alleyways that cluster higgledy-piggledy between the Old and New Forts, in the northern half of Corfu Town. It would surely take a lifetime fully to know your way around; new arrivals should simply try their best to keep some sense of direction – though the fun is in getting slightly lost and exploring what look like interesting side streets. Thirty years ago you might have seen donkeys clopping down some of these tiny passageways, their loads brushing against both walls, but now scooters buzz noisily through. Washing frequently hangs drying above your head, suspended across the wider streets, and you might see a housewife lowering a basket from her balcony to buy goods from a tradesman in the street below. There are tourist shops, bakeries, bars and other establishments all hidden away in the whitewashed alleys – so explore, but take care not to get totally lost.

UNDERNEATH THE ARCADES

The attractive arcaded streets of Corfu Town are not merely of architectural interest but also reflect the varied climate of this island. They provide protection from the hot sun of summer and from the heavy rains of winter. They shelter the coffee-drinkers and newspaper-readers whiling away the hours on the Listón, the tourists looking for postcards and souvenirs in the old town, and the local shoppers stocking up at bakers' and grocers' shops in the back streets.

Andivouniótissa Museum ★★

At the top of a flight of steps off Arseniou, and marked by a signpost, is an impressive **Byzantine** Museum. The small but very varied collection is well displayed in the Church of Panayía Andivouniótissa. Probably built in the late 15th century, the church was privately owned until 1979, when it was handed over to the Greek state on condition that it be turned into a museum. After repair work was carried out, the doors were first opened in 1984 by Melina Mercouri, the well-known actress who was then Greek Minister of Culture. By 1994 the final stage of restoration was completed, and a fuller new collection of icons put on display, many from the church itself. There are also old wall paintings.

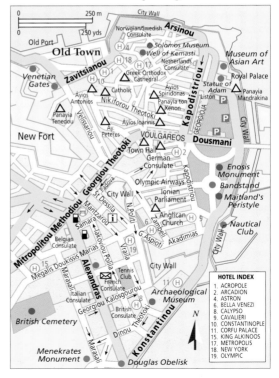

The collection of about 90 **icons** ranges in date from the 15th to the 19th centuries, most being from the 17th and 18th centuries. They include the usual goodly number of portraits of the saints, but it is the wide range of Biblical scenes, such as the *Stoning of St Stephen* and the *Washing of the Feet of Jesus,* that makes the collection particularly interesting. Most of the icons are as vividly colourful as the day they were painted. Around the walls of the church hang several very fine 'Scenes from the Old Testament' by the 17th- to 18th-century artist, Konstandinos Kontarines.

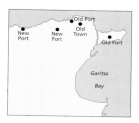

POET OF THE PEOPLE

Although he was born on Zákinthos in 1798, the poet Dionysios Solomos moved to Corfu in 1828 and stayed there until his death in 1857. He was at the heart of the intellectual revival on Corfu, and was especially popular as the first poet to use the ordinary spoken Greek for his work, not classical Greek as all writers before him had used. He believed that literature should be available for everyone to read, not just an élite. Every Greek now knows his work, for part of his poem *Hymn to Freedom* was set to music to become the Greek national anthem.

Enter the newly refurbished Byzantine Museum to admire Corfiot icons, paintings and carvings.

CORFU LITERARY SOCIETY

To the left of the Palace of St
Michael and St George is a
graceful building with an outside staircase leading to the
Corfu Literary Society.
Founded in 1836, the society
claimed most of Corfu's leading intellectual figures as
members. Though not generally open to the public, it frequently mounts exhibitions
and its collection of some
10,000 volumes about the
Ionian Islands can be consulted by genuine scholars. It
also houses collections of
maps, engravings, paintings,
photographs and newspa-
pers, and produces its own
publications.

Also important is the Cretan connection. During its
period of Venetian rule from the 13th to the 17th centuries, Crete was Greece's most important artistic centre.
As Corfu was a stopping-point on the route from Crete
to Venice, many of the most talented artists from the
Cretan School both visited and lived on the island for
short periods. Some of their works survived and are on
display here, as is explained in the informative notes (in
Greek and English) on the museum's walls.

Solomos Museum *

Also signposted just off Arseniou and close to the
Andivouniótissa Museum is the house where the Ionian
poet, **Dionysios Solomos** lived until his death in 1857.
Open on weekday evenings only, it will be of interest
mainly to enthusiasts and those with a good knowledge
of the Greek language – very little information is given in
anything other than Greek. There are old photographs
and oil paintings of the poet, an original manuscript, the
desk at which he wrote and other memorabilia, as well as
the chance to see inside his former home, but this museum is not likely to detain the average visitor for long.

Palace of St Michael and St George *

The Order of St Michael and St George was created in
1818, the year before the five-year construction of this
palace began, to honour British civil servants who had
served with distinction in Malta and the Ionian Islands.
The palace, built as a base for the Order and a residence
for the British High Commissioner, is constructed from
Maltese limestone. It stands at the northern edge of the
Esplanade, fronted by a statue of **Sir Frederick Adam**,
the British High Commissioner who pioneered the popularity of Paleokastrítsa and built the Mon Repos villa to
the south of Corfu Town.

GREEK POETIC TRADITION

Greece has a fine poetic tradition, with the rare distinction of two of its poets having won the Nobel Prize for
Literature, an honour indeed
for what is a minority language. Odysseus Elytis won
the prize in 1979, while
George Seferis had been
given the award in 1963. It
was yet another Nobel
Prizewinner, Rudyard Kipling,
who first translated Dionysios
Solomos' 'Hymn to
Freedom' into English.

In 1864, when the British left, the palace became a residence for the Greek royal family but later fell into ruin. It
was restored in the 1950s by the British Ambassador to
Greece, Sir Charles Peake, who was keen to see the palace
renovated and used in view of its British connections.

The west wing is now home to both the Tourist and Traffic Police, the eastern end of the building contains archive offices and a public library, and the splendid former State Rooms house the Museum of Asiatic Art. You may peer into several enticing senate and function rooms, but entry is not allowed. The well kept grounds around the palace make for a pleasant stroll away from the traffic.

The Palace of St Michael & St George houses government departments, police offices and a museum.

Museum of Asiatic Art ★★

The grandly restored State Rooms of the Palace of St Michael and St George house a collection of Asiatic art considered one of the finest in the world. The core of the museum, items from China, Japan, Tibet, Nepal and other Asian nations, was originally amassed by the Corfiot diplomat **Gregorios Manos**. His 10,000-piece collection was given to the state in 1927, and later bequests – from a Greek Ambassador to India, Japan and Korea and a Greek merchant based in the Netherlands – extended the scope of the collection. The result is a splendid and varied display, ranging from Buddhas to bronzes, from stonework to silk, and from armour to delicate porcelain and erotic Indian woodcarvings.

COLLECTOR EXTRAORDINARY

A passionate collector of oriental art, Gregorios Manos was born on Corfu and rose to become a diplomat. It was in 1919, when he was Greek Ambassador to Austria, that he offered his large collection to the state, on the condition that he could retire on a pension and spend the rest of his life as curator of the Museum of Sino-Japanese Art (as it then would have been called). Agreement was not reached until 1927, and sadly the following year Manos died in poverty, all his wealth having gone into his beloved art collection.

Cathedral *

Corfu's Orthodox Cathedral stands impressively at the top of a wide flight of steps near the Old Port. Built in 1577, it has been a cathedral only since 1841 and is known as the Cathedral of the Panayía Spiliótissa (Madonna of the Cave), or by the more familiar name of Mitrópolis (Cathedral). In fact it is dedicated to **St Theodora**, whose remains were brought to the island from Constantinople at the same time as those of St Spiridhon; her preserved body is kept in a silver coffin to the right of the altar. Theodora was a Byzantine Empress, revered for reinstating the worship of icons; like St Spiridhon, her only connection with Corfu is the presence here of her body, worshipped once a year when her coffin is opened. The Cathedral has the usual array of icons, the most notable being one of St George just inside the door. The interior is gloomily impressive, the three aisles making it broader and squatter than many Orthodox churches, but it cannot be described as either beautiful or of significant historical interest.

It is illegal to export genuine antique icons, but modern reproductions are of a very high standard and are an undeniably Greek memento.

Separate bell-towers, as here at the Church of St Spiridhon, are unusual in Greece but are a common feature on Corfu due to Italian influences.

Church of St Spiridhon **

At the end of the street named Spirídonos is the **holiest place on Corfu**. Here stands the church of St Spiridhon, its red-domed belfry the tallest on the island and a landmark as you head into the town from the Esplanade. The church was built in 1589 and dedicated to the saint whose mummified body it was intended to house. Spiridhon's remains had been wrapped in a sack of straw, tied to the back of a donkey and smuggled out of Constantinople in 1460 when the Turkish occupation was imminent.

Brought up as a shepherd on Cyprus, **Spiridhon** became first a monk then a bishop, and many minor miracles had been credited to him before his death in 350. When his body was later exhumed it had not decayed, and the saint's holy powers were reinforced. Chance led his remains to be taken to Corfu, but he quickly became the island's patron saint and has been revered for the last 500 years. Oddly enough, St Spiridhon's body remained the property of the descendants of the priest who had originally smuggled him out of Constantinople, only being handed to the church in 1927. Four times a year the saint's body – otherwise kept in its silver coffin to the right of the altar – is carried around the town in a procession.

THANKS TO ST SPIRIDHON

There are four days a year when the mummified remains of St Spiridhon are taken from his church and carried in procession around Corfu Town. It is something not to be missed, if your visit coincides with Palm Sunday, Easter Saturday, 11 August or the first Sunday in November. Each procession commemorates a different occasion on which the revered saint came to the help of the island: he has averted two plagues, one famine and one Turkish invasion attempt.

The Earl of Guilford, one of Corfu's most colourful characters.

THE EARL OF GUILFORD

One of the most un-Greek street names in Corfu Town is Guilford Street, named in honour of the fifth Earl of Guilford (1769–1828). He was a colourful British eccentric who lived on Corfu in the early 19th century, given to wearing golden wreaths and purple robes. He converted to the Greek Orthodox faith and reopened the Ionian Academy, which became the first university in modern Greece. Guilford is also remembered in a small park, named after him, just north of the entrance to the Old Fort. He sits there in stone, suitably robed.

Visitors to the church can sit and watch as a constant flow of visitors come to light candles and make their way to the coffin to kiss it and pray to St Spiridhon for help. Above the coffin hang dozens of silver thuribles (censers), while the church is crammed with silver candlesticks and votive offerings. The ceiling is decorated with some exquisite paintings.

Paper Money Museum **

Unlikely though it may seem, this is a fascinating museum. It is in Iroon Kypriakou Square, immediately south of the Church of St Spiridhon, housed above the **Ionian Bank** (constructed in 1846) in spacious rooms that were once the manager's residence.

The collection occupies several rooms, is open daily (morning only on Sundays) and has information in Greek and English. The museum has a complete collection of **Greek bank notes** up to the present day, and through these you can follow the flow of Corfu's more recent history. British pounds give way to drachmas; notes in Italian and German come into use during World War II to be followed by British pounds again, for military use only; then comes wild inflation, with notes up to 400 billion drachmas.

Upstairs is perhaps the most interesting part of the museum, where several rooms tell the full story of the 'simple' **production of a bank note**: which paper to use, how watermarks and other anti-forgery devices are implemented, and the complex procedures involved in the design and printing processes. The intricate work demanded of an engraver is given its full due, and the evolution of the tricky business of numbering notes is explained, as is the question of security at the printing works. Money will never seem the same again after a visit to this museum, claimed to be the only one of its kind in the world.

Old Fortress **

A single passageway connects the outcrop on which the Old Fortress stands with the eastern end of the Esplanade. Although the present Venetian remains were built in 1550, it is believed that there have been fortifications on this promontory since the 7th or 8th century. Until 1979 the area was used by the Greek Army, who then handed it over to the Greek Archaeological Service to begin restoration work. Access to much of the site was restricted until very recently, when a hefty admission fee was introduced for which visitors get little more than a splendid view over Corfu Town from the Castel Nuovo lighthouse at the very top. Beyond the rooftops of the town, the northeastern corner of the island can be clearly seen, with Mount Pandokrator standing supreme. Resorts such as Nissáki are plainly visible, while further to the right is the mainland of Albania and Greece. The southern suburbs of Corfu Town can be made out, with the airport runway and the magnificent southern sweep of the island off to the left.

The view apart, there is not much to detain the visitor. To the right of the entrance, around a corner, is a building which looks like the Parthenon's younger brother. This is the **Church of St George**, built by the British in 1840 for the use of the garrison which was then stationed here. It was badly bombed during World War II, then restored but later allowed to fall into further disrepair. It is now closed to visitors, a disharmonious eyesore.

To the left of the main entrance is the area where the summer **Sound and Light Shows** are held. These are preceded by an exhibition of traditional Ionian folk dances, and tickets can be booked for either or both shows. The

THE GREAT DEFENDER

Beside the entrance to the Old Fortress is the statue of Count John Matthias von der Schulenberg, whose most notable achievement on Corfu was to mastermind the defence against the attempted Turkish invasion of 1716. A Saxon mercenary in the pay of the ruling Venetian government, he was put in charge of the island's defence. On 8 August he led an army of the besieged from the Old Fortress in a surprise counter-attack which coincided with a violent storm (a helping hand from St Spiridhon perhaps). Three days later the Turks left the island.

Rock-solid for centuries, Corfu's Old Fortress is still being explored by archaeologists.

The Maitland Rotunda may appeal to the visitor, but ironically it stands opposite the statue of Ioannis Kapodistrias, who disliked Maitland and his British policies.

dance display normally starts at 21:00 on weekdays, 20:30 at weekends, the Sound and Light following 30 minutes later. Shows are given in English, Greek, Italian and French, but times and languages vary from year to year so check in advance.

The Esplanade ★★★

The open space directly in front of the Old Fortress, once a parade ground for Venetian and British soldiers, is said to be the largest square in Greece. To the north of the Esplanade, as it is called, is the Palace of St Michael and St George, while its western border is formed by the arcaded street known as the **Listón**, a favourite place for Corfiots to see and be seen. Built by a Frenchman on the lines of the rue de Rivoli in Paris, the elegant Listón is a terrace of coffee shops, with a few restaurants and souvenir shops for good measure. Your cup of coffee will be pricier here than anywhere else in town, but you are paying for the buzz and bustle.

Surrounded by palms, Judas trees and eucalyptuses, the Esplanade is a pleasant spot – even though it is one of the town's main parking areas. The northern half is given over to Corfu's famous **cricket pitch**, a somewhat less lethal use than the Venetians made of it – the area was a firing range. In the southern section there is a fountain, a **bandstand** regularly used for summer concerts, and a **rotunda**, built in 1816 in memory of the first British Lord High Commissioner to Corfu, Sir Thomas Maitland.

Across the main road from the rotunda is a statue to one of Corfu's most famous citizens, **Ioannis Kapodistrias**, who became the first president of modern Greece in 1827. He is buried in the Platitéra Monastery (page 46), and the **Kapodistrias Museum** has been created in his former home near the suburb of Evropouli.

The Town Hall *

This is one of Corfu Town's most appealing buildings, built by the Venetians as a single-storey assembly room in the late 17th century using **white marble** quarried near Mount Pandokrator. After use as a theatre and opera house, it eventually became the Town Hall in 1903 when the British added a second floor. In the attractive little square outside is good evidence of Corfu's diverse climate: on one side stands a palm tree, on the other a pine. Beyond are a fountain and café, and to one side is the Roman Catholic Cathedral of St James.

Archaeological Museum **

A few minutes' walk south of the town centre, along the sea front and just past the Hotel Corfu Palace, you will find this very pleasing modern museum in Vraila, a side street to the right.

As you climb the stairs to the first-floor rooms, look out for the **funerary stele** from the late 3rd or early 2nd century BC. It bears the inscription: 'You went 23 years old into the Underworld and left your mother Arpalis in mourning, your husband Aristandros widower and the children orphan. You chose for yourself the last sleep.' What family tragedy lies behind those enigmatic words?

Cricket match on the Esplanade.

FIND THE PRESIDENT

The museum dedicated to **Ioannis Kapodistrias**, Corfu's most famous political figure, is on the outskirts of Corfu Town and not easy to find. Ask for directions when you get to the suburb of Evropouli. Housed in the family residence, it contains a display of furniture, books and medals belonging to the great patriot who dedicated his early life to the cause of Greek independence and became Greece's first President. Kapodistrias was born into an aristocratic Corfiot family in 1776, and assassinated in Náfplion in the Peloponnese in 1831. The museum is open only on Wednesday and Saturday mornings.

Corfu's Town Hall (on the left) was an opera house at one time.

WINE, WOMEN . . .

As well as the major highlights described, the **Archaeological Museum** contains many minor delights as well. Look for the small statue of Aphrodite, the Goddess of Love, herself clothed but leaning against a statuette of a woman lifting her dress to reveal her naked body. A pediment from about 500BC, found near Kanóni, shows a carving of a Dionysian feast, with Dionysus himself holding a drinking horn full of wine.

Entering the central room you see at the far end a **carved crouching lion**, found near the Tomb of Menekrates in 1843, an important work from the 7th century BC. The wall behind this cleverly masks the entrance to the far room, which houses the museum's prime exhibit: **the Gorgon Frieze**. This makes a terrific impact as you turn the corner and see the huge frieze in all its terrifying glory, 17m long and 3m high with, at its centre, the grimacing figure of the Gorgon herself. Her waistband consists of two entwined, battling snakes and more serpents make up her hair. In fact the frieze is not consistent with the myth of the Gorgon: here she is is depicted flanked by her two offspring, Pegasus and Chrysaor, whereas mythology has it that her two children sprang from her blood when she was beheaded by Perseus. Little remains of the figure of Pegasus, though Chrysaor can be clearly seen holding a sword. The frieze is not intact, but the modern insertions to complete the impression do not detract from the most important archaeological find on Corfu, and one of the most powerful pieces of Greek sculpture outside the National Archaeological Museum in Athens. Dating from 590–580BC, it originally adorned the Temple of Artemis in ancient Kerkira. Other finds from the temple are displayed around the same room.

Don't let the domineering Gorgon distract you from the many smaller gems on display here, such as a fine bronze of a naked warrior and some clay theatrical masks. The museum also contains a comprehensive collection of some 10,000 coins, as well as bronzes and clay statuettes, many of them from the excavations on the Mon Repos estate, to the south of Corfu Town. There are lead tablets dating from the 6th and 5th centuries BC, inscribed with acknowledgements of debts, while the earliest exhibits include Neolithic fragments dating back to the 6th millennium BC.

Tomb of Menekrates *

Archaeology buffs will want to see this well preserved, roofed tomb of the 7th or 6th century BC – though it is unlikely to be the highlight of anyone's visit to Corfu. To find it, walk south along the sea front, past the Archaeological Museum, until you reach an obelisk at a junction of several roads. Go up Menekratous, which is to the left of the British Consulate building, until you come to the police station, whose grounds are the unlikely site of Menekrates' resting place: this area served as the cemetery of the ancient city of Kerkira. The circular structure is built of roughly dressed stones and has a conical roof which, though probably a later replacement, is almost certainly similar in appearance to the tomb's original roof.

A Corfiot consul on the Greek mainland, **Menekrates** was evidently a popular, or at least an important figure. After he drowned at sea, he was commemorated by this elaborate memorial, discovered in 1843. Its interest to historians is the fact that it is intact, but casual visitors can see only the couple of metres of it that are visible above the present ground level. Fenced off behind green railings, the tomb looks neglected, overgrown as it is with moss and surrounded by empty drink cans, sweet wrappers and other litter.

PEGASUS

The winged horse, Pegasus, was the son of the union between Poseidon and Medusa, the Gorgon. Shortly after being born Pegasus pawed the ground on Mount Helicon, which caused a spring to flow and this spring was later believed to be the source for all poetic inspiration. Pegasus eventually joined the Gods on Mount Olympus, where it was his duty to bring Zeus his lightning and thunderbolts.

British Cemetery **

From Platía Yioryiou Theotóki, more familiarly known
as San Rocco Square, the British Cemetery is five minutes' walk along the airport road, Dimoulitsa. A small
sign points you down a side street, past the mental hospital, into a green retreat. The door rings a bell as you
enter, bringing out the caretaker, a kindly man who
explains a little about the cemetery in broken English.

The secluded nature of the grounds is indicated by
the fact that over 25 species of orchid have been found
here, while goldcrests and great tits flutter and twitter in
the pine trees. The cemetery began as a burial place for
the British troops and other personnel who were stationed here, but has expanded to take in the British community generally, while one corner is given over to
German graves. Nearby is an orchard of apple and
orange trees, obviously well tended.

This is a moving as well as a
peaceful place. Some graves are
marked by simple wooden crosses –
'Harry Casson 1927–1983' – while
other memorials tell tragic stories of
mothers and babies dying in child-
birth. Young men lost in battle are
remembered here, notably in the
graves and memorial to 44 British
sailors who lost their lives to
Albanian mines while sailing in the
Corfu channel in 1946, the incident
that led to the severing of official
British relations with Albania (see
box, page 69).

Monastery of Platitéra *

A former convent, but more frequently referred to as a monastery,
this is open to the public but no
longer in use. To reach it, take a 10-
minute walk down Polikhroniou
Konstanda, off San Rocco Square.

This is a pleasant arcaded street, appetisingly filled with butchers, bakers and patisseries, though the traffic heading out for Paleokastrítsa can be very heavy. Where the road forks, take the right-hand option and you will see the monastery's red-topped bell tower ahead of you.

Enter the **courtyard** through a stone archway, between two palms – but heed the notice which says: 'You are kindly requested to enter this holy place properly dressed.' The well kept courtyard has bright white walls, green shutters and doors, a stone well and corners draped with bougainvillaea – an idyllic scene, though even here you don't quite escape the worst of the traffic noise.

It is more peaceful inside the church, but the dim light makes it difficult to appreciate the **fine icons** and paintings for which it is renowned, including several paintings by Koutouzis, a leading 18th-century artist, and some excellent ceiling paintings. The church was built in 1743, but virtually destroyed by French attacks on the island and rebuilt in 1801. Behind the ornate altarscreen, and not always accessible, is the surprisingly simple tomb of the great Corfiot hero, **Ioannis Kapodistrias**. If a priest is on duty and you express an interest in seeing the tomb, a small donation to the church's funds might secure you the privilege. Also buried here is Fotos Tzavellas, one of the leading figures in the Greek War of Independence.

Church of St Jason and St Sosipater ★★

In the southern suburb of Anemomylos, this is the only complete and authentic **Byzantine church** on Corfu and probably dates back to the 11th century, though it may be even earlier. The building is superb, in brick and red tile, with a bell tower and octagonal dome. Inside the entrance are two icons of the saints to whom it is dedicated, Jason of Tarsus and Sosipater of Iconium. Both were bishops and disciples of St Paul, and they are believed to have brought Christianity to Corfu in the 1st century AD, probably during the reign of the notorious Roman Emperor Caligula. They later suffered the unusual martyrdom of being incarcerated in a bronze bull and

Above: *Cool and quiet – the Monastery of Platitéra.* **Opposite:** *The British Cemetery is well maintained thanks to the War Graves Commission, which pays for its upkeep.*

GLADSTONE IN CORFU

The great Victorian statesman William Gladstone (1809–98) visited the Ionian Islands, then under British rule, in 1858 in order to discuss the dissatisfaction the islanders were feeling. There was at that time a great movement towards unification with mainland Greece, which had gained its own independence from the Turks in 1827. Gladstone became High Commissioner Extraordinary for a short period, but his proposals for reform were not accepted by the islanders and in 1863 formal moves were made for Britain to leave the Ionian Islands in favour of Greece.

The Church of St Jason and St Sosipater stands in the street which bears its name: Iassonios Sossipatriou.

burnt to death. The icons are believed to be the work of a 16th-century Cretan painter, Emanuel Tzanes, who also painted some of the other works around the walls. The very faded **wall paintings** also to be seen include an 11th-century fresco, just inside the entrance, showing a 10th-century Bishop of Corfu.

Mon Repos ★★

The area around the Mon Repos villa has an interesting history but offers little for the modern visitor to see. Less than an hour's walk south of Corfu Town along the sea road, this was the centre of the ancient city of Kerkira, and several of the old city's remains are visible but not visitable.

The 5th-century BC historian Thucidydes, in his account of the civil war on Corfu which broke out while the island's military forces were engaged in the Peloponnesian War (see page 12), refers to the city of Kerkira. Through him we know of the *agora* (market place), two harbours and three temples that then existed. The city spread over the greater part of the peninsula between the southern section of Garítsa Bay, which had the Harbour of Alkinoos, and Halikiopoulos Lagoon, with the Hyllaic Harbour. The northern extent of the ancient city can be seen in a fragment of its fortification wall preserved near the modern cemetery (it survived through being incorporated in a church).

The first thing you come to is the entrance to the Mon Repos beach, though access is restricted to the beach, bar and restaurant at this corner of the estate. The beach is not wonderful, but is packed at the height of summer, especially at weekends.

A short distance past the entrance to the beach are some of the remains of the **old city**, known as Paleopolis (literally, 'old city'). On the right is **Áyia Kerkira**, the city's church, an impressive ruin whose surviving walls, despite repeated destruction and rebuilding of the church, date back to the 5th century. It was built by Jovian, Bishop of Corfu, on the site of a pagan temple, which has been dated to the 5th century BC. The body of the church was destroyed in the 6th century, rebuilt,

This view from the Old Fortress shows how the modern town grew up near here for defence purposes, while the old city has since crumbled.

THE GORGONS

The best known characteristic of the Gorgons of Greek mythology is that with one glance they could turn a victim to stone. There were three Gorgons, the daughters of the sea god Phorcys and his wife, Ceto. These attractive creatures had teeth like tusks, snakes for hair, protruding tongues, ugly faces and golden scales. Of the three, Medusa is the only one not immortal, which means that her sisters, Stheno and Euryale, must still be around somewhere.

destroyed again in the 11th century, rebuilt, fell into disrepair, was renovated in 1537 and finally destroyed again in the bombings of World War II.

The road beside the church leads down to the few remains of the **Temple of Artemis**, from which came the Gorgon Frieze in the Archaeological Museum. You need to exercise your imagination to make sense of the various fragments of the old city which have been excavated. There are some remnants of the city walls, as well as part of the aqueduct and the old port – now well inland.

Opposite the Church of Áyia Kerkira are the walled entrance gates to the **Mon Repos villa**. This was built in 1824 by the British High Commissioner, Sir Frederick Adam, as a present for his wife. When the British left Corfu it fell into the hands of the Greek royal family, one of whose descendants was born there and was later to marry into the British royal family (see box opposite).

5th-century ruins of Áyia Kerkira, the church of the old city.

Sir Frederick Adam, pictured left, is the man responsible for the Mon Repos villa, which he built on the site of a pavilion which had been erected there by a Russian general.

The villa and grounds are not at present open to the public. The estate here is still owned by the Greek royal family, who were exiled after the monarchy was abolished in Greece by referendum in 1974. They may well never be allowed to return, unless they renounce their claims to the throne, which ex-King Constantine refuses to do. The future of their properties in Greece is, at the time of writing, subject to legal dispute.

Also opposite Áyia Kerkira is the site of Roman Baths, still being excavated. The road between the baths and the church leads up to the village of Analipsis. **Analipsis** means 'Ascension', and a good day to visit is the Feast of the Ascension, 40 days after Easter Sunday, when the whole of the village and seemingly half of Corfu Town turns out to celebrate the occasion. In the village is a path by the Taverna Kardaki which passes a spring gushing from the mouth of a Venetian stone lion's head in the rock face. This is the well-known **Kardaki water**, one sip of which – according to the inscription – will ensure that you completely forget your homeland.

Also in Analipsis are the remains of the **Temple of Kardaki**. This temple was discovered when the spring

stopped flowing in 1822, and the British Colonel in
charge set his men digging to find the cause of the block-
age. It was found that the hidden temple's altar had
slipped in the ground, diverting the flow of the stream;
the temple was excavated to restore the spring. Probably
dedicated to Apollo, this small temple was built late in
the 6th century BC and is the best preserved in the whole
of Corfu. It had 11 columns along each side and six at the
two ends. You can reach the temple by taking the left
fork where the main road divides into the one-way system, then taking the first left, leading uphill.

Further remains of the ancient city are hidden away in
the Mon Repos estate, including the ruins of Corfu's
largest temple, which was probably dedicated to Hera and
is known to have been reconstructed in the 4th century BC.

*At the busiest spot on
Corfu, Pondikoníssi, the
humble Greek fishing boat
still bobs in the waters.*

Kanóni ★★★

The two narrow roads through Analipsis to Kanóni, at the end of the peninsula south of Corfu Town, have been turned into a one-way system. The low road takes drivers past the smaller properties of this residential area, while the high road returns them through the more select part of Kanóni, where the luxurious Corfu Hilton is located.

Kanóni was once a pleasant retreat, a favoured picnic spot. Today it is a select address for Corfiot residents and also the hub of a separate tourist development, poised between Corfu Town and the next coastal resorts to the south, Pérama and Benitses. There are several hotels, apartment blocks, restaurants, souvenir shops and cafés, and it would be a good base for a holiday, with easy access to Corfu Town and the eastern coast, if it were not for one considerable drawback – it is under the **airport** flight path. Watching planes come and go while sitting over a cup of coffee is pleasant enough for an hour or so; whether you would want to endure it for two weeks is another matter.

The daily assault on the ears from the aeroplanes bringing invading holiday-makers is appropriate, as Kanóni means 'battery'. The name comes from the days when the French installed an artillery battery here in 1798, and a large cannon from that time remains in the little square surrounded by shops and cafés, one of which offers an unrivalled view of the most photographed sight in Corfu, if not Greece – the islands of Pondikoníssi and Vlachérna out in the bay. The café's prices are tailored accordingly.

A regular bus service runs from Corfu Town to the tip of the Kanóni peninsula, but if you enjoy walking it's not more than an hour or so's stroll into the centre of Corfu Town. Certainly the British who used to favour this spot during their 50-year rule on Corfu would walk out to it in the evenings just as the Greeks today enjoy their Volta. In fact the writer and artist Edward Lear complained on one of his visits to the island and refused 'pottering to the one-gun battery'.

PROGRESS?

Kanóni is typical of the way Corfu has changed over the years, particularly since the 1950s when the numbers of visitors started to increase. Many quiet fishing villages have gone, to be replaced by rows of hotels, villas, tavernas, bars, discos and tourist shops. That is not to say that these changes should only be lamented, as those fishing and farming villages were poor as well as picturesque. The boom in tourism has brought prosperity to many, and convenience to others by way of such 'luxuries' as water and electricity supplies.

Pondikoníssi ★★★

Pondikoníssi or Mouse Island is the name of the further of the two islets in the bay below Kanóni, though it is sometimes incorrectly applied to the closer one. The latter, joined to the mainland by a causeway, is called Vlachérna.

On **Vlachérna** an immaculately white convent is flanked by a single lofty tree standing taller even than the bell tower. Fishing boats are tied along the causeway, and with the blue sea, bobbing boats, white church, green tree, the island of Pondikoníssi behind and the mountain slopes of southern Corfu in the distance beyond, it is little wonder that so much photographic film has been exposed here.

What the photographs never show, of course, is the car park that has been built to accommodate the endless visitors, and the rather scruffy strip of land to the right with, about 400m away, the start of the airport runway that was built on the lagoon. Nonetheless, Vlachérna and Pondikoníssi do provide a unique and glorious view for the start and end of your visit to Corfu.

Boats from Vlachérna make the journey to and from Corfu Town hourly in summer, and some will take interested visitors on the short trip across to **Pondikoníssi**. Here a solitary church hides among the vaguely mouse-shaped trees, but the most interesting thing about the islet is mythical. It is said to be the petrified ship which, in Homer's *Odyssey*, was wrecked by Poseidon, causing Odysseus to be washed up on the shores of Scheria. However, other towns in Corfu, such as Ermónes and Paleokastrítsa, also claim to be Odysseus' landing point on the island.

Vidos Island ★

This island, prominent in the waters of Corfu harbour, has been a wildlife sanctuary since 1993. It is a more peaceful place today than in the past. Once the hunting preserve

of a Venetian count, it was occupied no less than three times over the centuries by forces attempting to take Corfu, who used it as a firing base. Later the British turned it into a penal settlement and later still it became a cemetery (see box on page 19). Now on Vidos, Kerkira Bird and Wildlife Sanctuary looks after abandoned and injured birds and animals, such as buzzards, harriers, seagulls, otters, herons and swans. Visitors may adopt an animal if they wish, which commits them to paying its food bill and entitles them to reports on its health. Visits to the island can also be arranged (tel 0661-32711).

To the east of Vidos is the tiny islet of Lazaretto, also referred to as Gouvion and more clearly visible from the resort of Kondókali (see next chapter). Lazaretto may look attractive but it has a sad history, having been used in the Venetian period as a quarantine station for ships thought to be carrying the plague that badly affected Corfu. In more recent times, during the Greek Civil War which followed World War II, Lazaretto was used as a place of execution. Every 27 May a pilgrimage is made to the island by those families who lost loved ones, and flowers are placed in the bullet holes in the wall where the prisoners were shot.

Above: *The keen photographer will be challenged to find a new angle on this most photographed of scenes, below Kanóni.*
Opposite: *Peace and tranquillity in the convent on the island of Vlachérna.*

WHITE EGRETS

The airport runway, built into the Halikiopoulos Lagoon close to Corfu Town Centre, is good news for visitors and the tourist trade, but bad news for the white egret. This graceful bird sometimes winters in the lagoon and, with an estimated population of only 200 individuals, it is one of the most endangered species in Europe. About half the population has been counted on the lagoon at one time.

Corfu Town at a Glance

Best Times to Visit

In **May–June** and **September–October** the sun is likely to be shining and the streets less crowded than at peak times, yet everywhere will be open. September sees the annual Corfu Festival, with concerts, ballet, opera and drama. For local colour, visit at **Easter** (note that the Orthodox festival rarely coincides with Easter in western Europe), or at the time of one of **St Spiridhon's processions** (see page 39). **Carnival**, just before Lent, is also a colourful event.

Getting There

The **international airport** (tel 0661-30180) is about 1.5km (one mile) south of the town centre and offers tourist information, car hire, snacks, bar, duty-free shopping and currency exchange (open 09:00-02:00 provided international flights are expected). Otherwise, visitors should have some Greek currency available for a taxi as there is no public bus service into Corfu Town. However, a courtesy bus meets Olympic flights and takes passengers to the Olympic office on Kapodistriou.

Getting Around

Corfu Town is small enough to see **on foot**, with the occasional taxi if visiting, say, Kanóni, though this is also served by bus. The main **taxi rank** is on the Esplanade (tel

0661-39926), with others on Theotóki (tel 0661-39911) and San Rocco Square (tel 0661-30383), and smaller ranks elsewhere. **Buses** serving the town and its suburbs can be picked up at the Esplanade and San Rocco Square. Unless you are visiting the rest of the island, **car hire** is best avoided because of parking and driving difficulties in the busy, narrow streets.

Where to Stay

Note: all hotels in Kanóni suffer some airport noise during the day

Luxury

Corfu Hilton: in Kanóni, set in woodland, with own beach, pool, bars and recommended restaurant; complimentary bus service to Corfu Town, tel 0661-36540, fax 0661-45933.

Corfou Palace: elegant hotel overlooking Garítsa Bay with beautiful gardens and views across to the Greek mainland; indoor and outdoor pools plus separate children's pool, sun terraces and many other facilities tel 0661-39485, fax 0661-31749.

Mid-range

Arion: fairly large hotel out of the centre, in the suburb of Anemómilos (the Mon Repos area), with gardens, swimming pool and sun terrace. Public bus to town centre stops outside. B grade, tel 0661-37950.

Bella Venezia: smartly restored old mansion, quiet

but central and reasonably priced; C grade, tel 0661-44290, fax 0661-20708.

Cavalieri Hotel: modern façade hides old-style hotel with character, near Esplanade and sea front. No swimming pool, roof garden with views; A grade, tel 0661-39041.

Corfu Divani Palace: A grade hotel with own pool and disco in Kanóni, tel 0661-38996.

Hotel Royal: reasonably priced and ornately decorated C grade hotel in Kanóni with three eye-catching linked swimming pools, tel 0661-35343.

Marina Beach: close to the Mon Repos Lido, this B grade hotel is 3km (2 miles) out of town. It has a garden and a restaurant serving local dishes, tel 0661-32783.

Budget

Hotel Calypso: faded but comfortable C grade hotel with great character and very friendly owners, once a favourite haunt of Lawrence Durrell, tel 0661-30723.

Hotel Ionion: C grade hotel below the New Fortress and overlooking the harbour; drab exterior hides pleasant rooms, all ensuite, tel 0661-30628.

Where to Eat

Only the smarter Corfu restaurants take telephone bookings; where no number is given you cannot reserve by phone.

Argo, Ethnikis Antistasseos

Corfu Town at a Glance

(New Port): good seafood, though expensive, tel 0661-24938.

Averof, Prosalendou (Old Port): there's good local food at this well-known restaurant; often very busy, tel 0661-31468.

Il Giardino: almost opposite the Archaeological Museum, expensive and smart Tuscan restaurant, tel 0661-30723.

Grill Room Chrissomallis, Nikiforou Theotóki: honest-to-goodness Greek taverna with no frills but good value typical Greek dishes and friendly service.

Hrissi Kardia, Sevastianou: noisy taverna with good grilled food; always full of locals.

Orestes, Xenofontos Stratigou (New Port): good fish and seafood, as well as local dishes; you can eat in the garden, tel 0661-35664.

Poulis, Spirou Arbanitaki: tucked away on a side street off Theotóki is this typical Corfiot grill.

Rex: opened in 1932, with Corfiot, Greek and international dishes and fine wine list, tel: 0661-39649.

Spiros, Guilford Street: busy Corfiot grill-cum-takeaway to southeast of Town Hall.

Venetian Well, Kremasti Square (near the Cathedral): delightful atmosphere and excellent, good-value Corfiot food with a menu that changes daily, tel 0661-44761.

Xenikhtis, Potamou Street:

an international menu is served here in the suburb of Mandouki beside the Monastery, tel 0661-24911.

Yisdhakis, Solomou (off N Theotóki): serves authentic local food.

The smartest area for cafés is the Listón. For a more authentic local atmosphere try the establishments in and near San Rocco Square.

TOURS AND EXCURSIONS

A trot round Corfu Town in a horse and buggy is a popular option among holiday-makers. Corfu Town is also the place to plan your ferry trips to other islands.

Airtours Greece, tel 0661-32182/39466, fax 0661-23604.

All Ways Travel, tel 0661-33955/45516, fax 0661-30471.

Corfu Holidays, tel 0661-36241/31226/31386, fax 0661-43003.

Corfu Infotravel, tel 0661-25933/41550/25792, fax 0661-23829.

Style Travel, tel 0661-45503/32541, fax 0661-30658.

Wonder Travel, tel 0661-35329, fax 0661-30529.

USEFUL CONTACTS

Ambulance, tel 166
Bus Timetables, tel 0661-31595 (local/Benitses/Dassía), or 0661-39862 (rest of island).
Corfu Climbing Club, tel 0661-95022/40911/39481.
Corfu General Hospital, Polikhroniou Konstanda, tel 0661-45811.
Corfu Tennis Club, Romanou (near Archaeological Museum), tel 0661-37021.
Live entertainment: Greek folk dancing at Old Fort, tel 0661-30360, 39730; *bouzoúki* music at Esperides nightclub, Kerkira Golf Hotel, Alikes (north of town), tel 0661-31785.
Ferry Timetables, tel 0661-32655.
Municipality of Corfu Tourist Information Offices are situated at the New Port (tel 0661-28509), with information kiosks on the Esplanade and San Rocco Square.
NTOG, tel 0661-37638.
Police, tel 100
Port Police, tel 0661-32655.
Post Office, main branch on Alexandras, open Monday-Saturday, 07:30-20:00, tel 0661-39604.
Tourist Police, tel 0661-39503.

CORFU	J	F	M	A	M	J	J	A	S	O	N	D
MAX °C	14	14	16	19	24	28	31	31	28	23	19	15
MIN. °C	5	6	7	9	13	16	18	18	16	13	10	7
Hours of Sun Daily	5	6	7	7	9	10	11	12	9	6	4	3
RAINY DAYS	17	15	15	12	9	5	2	3	7	12	16	18
RAINFALL mm	153	140	107	64	38	12	7	17	84	152	193	185

3
The Northeast

The sweep of coast stretching from the northern suburbs of Corfu Town to the resorts that nestle below Mount Pandokrator is the most touristy area of the island, with boisterous towns where anything goes in summer (**Ipsos**, **Pyrgi**) and more family-based resorts (**Komméno**, **Gouvía**). Inland, the reconstructed 'old' village of **Daniliá** attracts visitors with its glimpses of a past Corfu and its lively Greek evenings as well as a chance to buy handicrafts and other souvenirs. At the end of this stretch are the lovely small resort of **Kalámi**, associated with the Durrell brothers, and quiet **Kouloúra**. Beyond Kouloúra, the coast road turns north and heads inland, skirting the mountain that dominates this region, rugged **Mount Pandokrator**. Minor but perfectly drivable roads go through mountain villages almost to the summit, and the green slopes are rich in plant life, particularly orchids

The resorts around the bulge that forms the far northeast of the island have a different feel from the holiday centres lining the bay north of Corfu Town and forming an almost unbroken chain. **Kassiópi**, for example, though it has bars and souvenir shops, is a genuine – and attractive – Corfiot town. There is fine scenery and good walking too. This area offers great variety – the longest single stretch of **golden sand** on the island, the wetlands of the **Andinióti lagoon** for birdwatchers, busy resorts such as **Akharávi** and **Ródha** – and will probably appeal to those who wish to go out and about while also enjoying watersports and some evening entertainment.

CORFU / ALBANIA / ● Corfu Town / Ionian Sea

DON'T MISS

*** Kalámi: village with literary connections
*** Kouloúra: peaceful with a delightful harbour
*** Danilia: unashamedly commercial folk village
*** Mount Pandokrator: Corfu's highest peak with magnificent views
*** Ródha, for a beautiful stretch of beach
** Barbáti: in a beautiful setting under Pandokrator
** Kassiópi: a lively holiday resort, but still very Corfiot
** Andinióti Lagoon, for a glimpse of Corfu's wildlife.

Opposite: *Barbáti's magnificent setting is typical of northeast Corfu.*

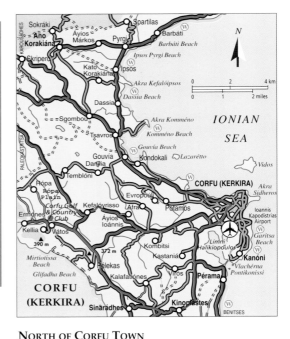

NORTH OF CORFU TOWN
Kondókali *

Lying only about 6km (4 miles) north of Corfu Town, Kondókali is – not surprisingly – heavily developed for tourism. It is situated in an ideal spot, at one end of the grand sweep of **Gouvía Bay** with its offshore island of Lazaretto (see page 55) and, beyond that, the mountainous Albanian mainland. A promontory juts out to sea, helping to provide shelter for the yachts in the marina here. Part of the headland is given over to the Luxury class **Kondókali Bay Hotel**, with its own sports facilities, saltwater swimming pool and nightclub.

The village is off the main coastal road, with bars, tavernas and shops lining its own main street. Several smaller streets lead down to thin strips of **pebbly beach**, packed in summer and providing a wealth of **watersports**. The bay is very sheltered thanks to the two pincers of land that protect it from the Ionian Sea, and the

*Daniliá village may be pur-
pose-built, but its shapes
and colours are traditional.*

water is quite shallow here. With several buses per day
to and from Corfu Town, Kondókali makes a good spot
for those who want a lively holiday with lots to do, and
who don't mind the fact that there is little real Greek feel
to the place.

Daniliá ★★★

Built in the hills behind Kondókali and Gouvía, this folklore village was created by a Greek family to give an
impression of Corfiot village life 200 years ago. It is reasonably effective, given the fact that its streets are
jammed with thousands of visitors during the day, while
in the evening it attracts hundreds more as a popular

venue for the organized **'Greek night'**, with food, wine flowing freely, folk music and dancing as well as more contemporary floor shows.

The houses are built in traditional Corfu style, partly from materials taken from old buildings that were falling into disrepair elsewhere on the island. There are arcaded stretches of street, Venetian shutters and even washing drying between them. In the houses you will find **local craftsmen** displaying their skills at pottery, wood-carving and other crafts, and such goods are on sale in the many shops. A **ceramics factory** offers an opportunity to buy at factory prices. There is also a small **museum** with a display of traditional costumes, domestic scenes and agricultural implements.

Gouvía **

A couple of kilometres beyond Kondókali, Gouvía stands in an attractive spot at the heart of its own natural harbour. There are splendid views out to sea and of Mount Pandokrator to the north, where Corfu's coast swings dramatically eastwards below the peak. This is more of a **family resort** than Kondókali, quieter and with safe bathing from a curving sand and shingle beach, which offers the usual facilities of sunbeds and umbrellas for hire, and popular watersports such as paragliding and water-skiing. Like Kondókali, Gouvía has its own recently completed **marina** at the southern end of the village – work began 20 years ago under a scheme by the Greek tourist authorities to improve the quality of some of its marinas to international standards and work at Gouvía was due for completion in 1994. The Turkish troops of Suleiman the Magnificent needed no such facilities in 1537 when they attempted to invade Corfu at this point on the coast. Close to the marina are the remains of a Venetian arsenal and shipyard, built after the Turkish siege of 1716. Now roofless, its massive arches nevertheless evoke the arrogance of a power that had dominated the Mediterranean for centuries. In more recent times, Gouvía Bay was used as a naval base by another nation – the French fleet was here in World War I.

Komméno **

One of the lesser-known resort areas along this stretch of coast, and not even mentioned in some guidebooks, Komméno appeals to some people for its very **lack of tourist facilities** – at least compared to the other resorts nearby. It clusters around its own small bay, facing Kondókali on the opposite side of the larger Gouvía Bay. It has several small sandy beaches, which have been purpose made, some for the use of guests at the luxury **Astir Palace Hotel** on one of the cape's headlands. There are other hotels and some shops and tavernas scattered around, but Komméno is a cape and a bay rather than an actual old village – one of the reasons development has been slow. Komméno lies well away from the busy coastal road, surrounded by woodland; visitors need to have the use of a car or be prepared to walk 3km (2 miles) to Gouvía or 2km (just over a mile) to Dassia for access to buses into Corfu Town.

Watersports centres, like this one at Dassia, can be found in most of the major resorts.

BEST BEACHES

** Gouvía: a curve of sand
and shingle with safe bathing
** Komméno: offering a
choice of small sandy bays
** Ipsos and Pyrgi: lovely
'Golden Mile' of beach if you
don't mind company
** Áyios Spiridhon: large
sandy beach, quiet in places
but can be busy in season
** Ródha: a bay large
enough to escape the
crowds.
* Barbáti: stony beach, but in
an impressive setting below
Mount Pandokrator
* Kamináki: shingle beach in
a typical Greek setting

Dassia *

Dassia is an increasingly popular resort. Large though
the beach is, it still becomes very full indeed at the height
of the season, with more and more visitors arriving as
new hotels are built year after year. The two Chandris
hotels which for a long time dominated the resort, with
over 1000 beds between them, have recently been joined
by several others, adding another 1500 beds. Furnished
apartments and rented rooms also abound. With **discos**,
bars and **bustle**, it is not a resort for those who like peace
and quiet and an early night.

Most of the hotels, bars, tavernas, cafés, supermarkets and souvenir shops run along either side of the busy
coastal road, which cuts straight through the village and
could be a drawback for families. However, the long
strand of mostly **shingle beach** is away from the road,
reached down narrow alleys and backed by olive groves,
which help cut down the noise of the passing traffic. The
word *dasos*, meaning 'forest', indicates the **wooded
nature** of this region. The beach turns sandy at its northern end, where Club Méditerranée have set up their
bamboo huts with a sign warning casual strollers that the
facilities are private. The public facilities at Dassia
include **watersports** galore, with no less than three
water-skiing schools. For a change of scene, boat trips
from the several landing stages are also available.

Ipsos and Pyrgi **

If you're looking for good old-fashioned fun in the sun,
this could be the place for you. Once separate resorts,
Ipsos and Pyrgi have now merged, giving an indication
of their recent rates of expansion. They share a long
curve of beach, a mix of sand and shingle, giving the
resorts the title of '**The Golden Mile**'. At the height of
the summer they are patronised almost exclusively by
young, single Europeans, whose idea of a good holiday
is to drink all night and spend the next day recovering.
The British are very much in evidence, with British pubs,
British breakfasts and fish and chip shops outnumbering
the more traditional Greek places.

YES AND NO

In Greek *ne* means 'yes' and
ochi 'no' (pronounced *neh*
and *oh-kee* or *oh-she* respectively). Further confusion can
be caused by a common
Greek gesture that can look
like a nodding of the head in
agreement: a backward
movement of the head with a
raising of the eyebrows,
sometimes with an added
tutting sound, in fact means
a definite 'no'.

In early and late season, when there is room on the beach and the night noise is not quite so relentless, Ipsos and Pyrgi make a **good base** for those who don't necessarily fall into the young and single category. There are plenty of facilities, Corfu Town is only 14km (9 miles) away with regular bus services, the area behind the resorts is filled

with pleasant paths through olive groves, and beyond these the slopes of Mount Pandokrator rise to give a glorious backdrop to this sweep of beach.

One drawback at **Ipsos** is that the main road runs right alongside the beach. Behind the southern stretch of this beach, a few old cottages and a church remain to remind people of the tiny settlements which used to be here. **Pyrgi** to the north has the sandier part of the beach.

Above: *Ipsos harbour, where you will find everything from rowing boats to luxury yachts.*
Below: *While the beaches may be packed, the back streets of Ipsos still have quiet picturesque corners.*

The resort marks, for the moment, the end of the near-continuous spread of development on this stretch of coast north of Corfu Town. Inland the road leads up to **Áyios Markos**, a village devastated in the 1950s by a landslide. Homeless families were given land further down towards Pyrgi and resettled in what became New Áyios Markos. This settlement became the nucleus of the modern resorts, a different world from the timeless

Expect to pay a few hundred drachmas to rent a sunbed for the day.

rusticity only a short distance inland from the beach, the bars and the discos. Many old houses remain in the still picturesque upper village and there are two old churches, one of the 11th and the other of the 16th century, the latter's walls covered with frescoes also from the 16th century. From here you have a wonderful view back down over Ipsos Bay. Just beyond Pyrgi, a road branches off to the left from the main coastal road and corkscrews its way up towards the top of Mount Pandokrator.

Most summer visitors sunbathe and roister unaware of the history of the two villages, but in the past the 'Golden Mile' has witnessed scenes rather different from those of today. As at Gouvía, the Turks attempted to invade here, in 1537 and again in 1716. The name Pyrgi means 'tower', referring to the towers built behind the coast to give advance warning of any potential Turkish attacks from the occupied mainland. Ipsos ('height') is said to have been named to fool the Turks into believing that it might not be a good place to try to capture. If invaders came today, the boats would have a problem getting through the water-skiers, paragliders, pedaloes, windsurfers and swimmers, let alone up the beach where sunbathers lie cheek by jowl.

SEA HAZARDS

The very few beaches on Corfu with difficult currents are marked as such, and anyone ignoring advice about swimming conditions does so at their own risk. There are occasional invasions of jellyfish, but because of their large numbers they tend to be easily seen. Harder to spot are the spiky sea urchins, which haunt rocky areas. Sea urchin spines in your foot are painful but not fatal. The pain can be alleviated by the application of urine!

Barbáti **

Though only about two kilometres (just over a mile) beyond Pyrgi, Barbáti is a very different place. It is much more of a **family resort** and ideal for those who prefer a quieter holiday. That is not to say that facilities are non-existent – there are plenty of **watersports** on offer, sunbeds for hire and boat trips to take. There are simply far fewer of them, while the village itself has only a handful of souvenir and other shops. Barbáti has a more **impressive setting** than the resorts to the south, with the slopes of Mount Pandokrator rising through olive groves almost immediately behind the white-stone beach, which turns to a sandy shingle where the water laps.

The main road is some way above the village, while the gently shelving beach and the sheltered nature of the bay mean that the bathing is fairly safe – all 'pros' for families with children. There is plenty of shade under the trees, which reach almost to the water's edge in places, and which tend to hide the few hotels and other buildings around.

At Nissáki boats will take you on trips along the coast, often with a barbecue picnic included.

Nissáki *

By the time it reaches Nissáki, the coast road is well above the several beaches which make up this **small fishing village**. Access is on steep tracks down through the olive groves. The main bars and restaurants and the few shops are along the main road, while the principal beach is of shingle and has a few tavernas. Other quiet beaches and private coves are accessible if you don't mind a short walk and a scramble down goat tracks to get to them.

Even though Nissáki is smaller and quieter than other resorts, it is a rare place on this part of the coast which does not offer a range of watersports, and this is no exception. There is windsurfing, paragliding and water-skiing, while boats are available for private hire as well as offering organized trips to other resorts along the coast. Corfu Town, 22km (14 miles) away, can be reached by boat or by the regular bus service which takes 40 minutes. There are four buses daily in high summer, and taking the first bus in and the last bus back allows you at least five hours in Corfu Town. By the bus stop is a minor road marked Viglatsouri, which eventually leads to the **deserted village of Sinie**s – a stimulating but tough walk.

Kaminaki *

Although the relentless holiday development peters out at Pyrgi, Kaminaki is the first village along this coast where a sense of the real **pre-tourism Corfu** prevails. Access is down a snaking road off the main coast road, and the bulk of what little accommodation the village has to offer is in self-catering apartments hidden away on the thickly wooded slopes. Many of these are sold as part of a package holiday, so potential visitors should be aware of the shortage of casual 'rooms to rent'.

Even quiet resorts like Agni are likely to throb with the noise of motor boats as people try out the many water sports on offer.

The beach here is of fine white shingle, with a solitary taverna, **Spiro's**, serving Greek dishes made by the owner's mother. There are a few windsurfers and boats for hire, and water-skiing lessons are available. A couple of shops and another taverna slightly away from the beach just about complete the facilities. The bay here is close to the northern end of the beach at Nissáki, and nearby is a Club Méditerranée camp. A track along the coast leads north to the next resorts: Agni, Kalámi and Kouloúra.

Boats are often the easiest way to reach small bays, such as this one at Agni.

THE ANGLO-ALBANIAN INCIDENTS

In 1945–6 a series of battles took place in the Corfu Channel between the British Royal Navy and the communist forces of Albania, who had taken control of the country after wartime liberation. The channel was heavily mined by the Albanians, and the Royal Navy suffered its heaviest casualties after the end of World War II, particularly in 1946 when 44 sailors died in a single incident: they are buried with a memorial in the British Cemetery in Corfu Town. On 9 April 1949, the International Court of Justice of the United Nations gave its first decision, when it held Albania responsible for these incidents and awarded damages to Britain.

Agni ★

Agni is reached by a very steep path down from the main road, which at this point is about 600m (2000ft) above the coast. This naturally deters many Greek drivers, who are not given to walking long distances in order to find places to swim and eat. Agni still attracts plenty of visitors, however, as holidaymakers come on foot from along the coast, and others arrive by excursion boat or in their private yachts. The handful of **tavernas** along the steeply shelving pebble beach have good reputations, and one, Taverna Nikolas, offers a service whereby diners are collected in its boat and returned home later in the evening.

The dramatic colours of Corfu in summer are shown in the harbour at Kouloúra: bright whites, deep blues and verdant greens.

THE DURRELL BROTHERS

Born in India in 1925, Gerald Durrell developed his interest in nature during his childhood on Corfu. His account of those days, *My Family and Other Animals*, became an international best-seller. Gerald went on to study zoology, became a zoo keeper and animal collector and was a dedicated conservationist. His Channel Island zoo, the Jersey Zoological Park, and his Jersey Wildlife Preservation Trust, have been responsible for the captive breeding and re-release into the wild of many endangered species. Gerald Durrell died in 1995.

As well as appearing in Gerald's book as the artistic elder brother, Lawrence Durrell (1912–1990) wrote his own memoir of Corfu life, *Prospero's Cell*, an atmospheric, vivid and impressionistic book. His fame was to be as a poet and novelist and he is remembered especially for the brilliant and sensuous *Alexandria Quartet*.

Kalámi ✦✦✦

The main road turns right into Kalámi, and left into the neighbouring resort of Kouloúra. Kalámi's claim to fame in English-speaking circles is **the Durrell connection**. Lawrence Durrell wrote *Prospero's Cell*, in 1939, in the White House at the southern end of the bay, now a taverna with some rooms to rent, including the one in which Durrell worked and which still contains his desk. Some sources mistakenly claim that this is the 'white house' in which the whole Durrell family lived, as described in Gerald Durrell's *My Family and Other Animals*. However, the 'Snow-white Villa' of that book is described as being 'perched on a hill-top among olive trees' – clearly not the White House at Kalámi, which stands at the water's edge and which Lawrence Durrell rented for a while with a friend.

Literary connections apart, Kalámi is a delightful small resort, its curving bay of coarse sand and shingle fringed at the back with cypress and olive trees. During the day it is popular with boat excursions and car drivers, but in the evening it quietens down, though there is often **Greek dancing and music** at one or more of the handful of beach tavernas. For a small resort, its facilities are quite good, with car, bike, sea scooter and boat hire all available. Outside July and August, it would make the ideal spot for those who want a quiet, **genuinely Corfiot resort**. Buses run to Corfu Town from the Kalámi-Kouloúra junction.

Kouloúra ★★★

The final resort along this coast, before the road stops heading east and swings to the north, is even less busy than Kalámi. Kouloúra has a much smaller beach, of rocks and pebbles, without even sunbeds for hire. Life tends to centre on the **attractive old harbour**, with its solitary taverna and a few boat trips on offer. The small harbour is surrounded by cypress trees and forms almost a complete circle in the larger circle of the bay: Kouloúra means 'ring' (there is also a round biscuit called a *Kouloúra*), the name deriving from the shape of the bay. Beyond the bay lies the mainland of Albania, only a couple of kilometres distant at this point.

Kouloúra's rounded harbour still has as many local fishing boats as those bringing in day-trippers to this idyllic place.

THE FAR NORTHEAST
Mount Pandokrator ***

At 906m (2972ft), Mount Pandokrator may not be exceptionally high compared to peaks on the Greek mainland
or on other larger Mediterranean islands, but to reach the
summit is still an achievement and not a trip to be
undertaken casually. The reward is a **stunning view**,
over the bay to Corfu Town in the south, across the
straits to Albania in the east, and even to Corfu's offshore islands in the distant northwest. Away to the
south, you might be able to see the small islands of Paxos
and Antipaxos, and it is said that on an exceptionally
clear day the Italian mainland is visible. On the way up
you may see some of Pandokrator's many **orchids**, such
as the easily recognisable bee and monkey orchids. The
many other flowers, including purple crocuses and gold-
en-headed thistles, attract large numbers of butterflies.
Unfortunately there are also multitudes of flies in places,
so go prepared with insect repellent .

The mountain can be approached from near Pyrgi, or
from a turn-off marked 'Loutsés' roughly midway

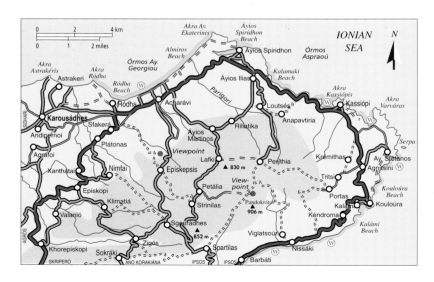

between Kassiópi and Akharávi. The road that goes to the summit is very rough and dusty; while it can be tackled in a sturdy four-wheel drive vehicle, the average visitor in a hire car would be better advised to leave the vehicle in the village of Períthia, just short of the summit, and finish the journey on foot. Directions

are not really necessary, as the top is crowned by an **old monastery** and a rather more visible modern radio mast. In summer, you should take plenty of water and try to avoid the midday sun. In spring or autumn – and certainly in winter – don't attempt to go up if there are clouds around: the weather can change quickly on Corfu, so you should avoid the risk of getting lost in descending mist. In any case, always let someone know where you are going.

Although it takes a little effort to get to the top, the views from Mount Pandokrator make the trek worthwhile.

Áyios Stéfanos *

A fishing village slowly developing into a resort, Áyios Stéfanos is a couple of kilometres off the main road, down a smooth but steeply winding road which tends to deter land-based visitors. However, day-trippers arrive by boat, so the idyll can be disturbed at any time during the day; the nightlife, on the other hand, being limited to a few bars and a handful of tavernas, will hardly attract the hordes. The main beach is large and pebbly and offers some watersports; for those who like even more **peace and privacy** there are quieter coves within walking distance.

At this point Corfu is at its closest to Albania, 1.7km (1 mile) away. Boats make the journey to Corfu Town, or you can walk up to the main road and flag down a bus. Greek bus drivers will happily stop to let people on and off even if there is no official stop.

Boats are a way of life on all Greek islands, used for fishing, tourist trips or simply for transport.

Kassiópi ★★

Although Kassiópi is now a bustling holiday town it has not yet lost sight of its Corfiot origins, and tourist and traditional aspects manage to rub along together. **Fishing boats** still go out from the harbour each night, while the bars and discos are pulsating. Most of the development is in villas rather than hotels, so the attractive setting – between two headlands, below the mountain slopes and with views across the sea to Albania – has not been swamped with white concrete blocks.

The name is made up of *kassi* (meaning 'border'), and *opia* ('look-out point'). The Phaeacean god, Kassios Zeus, was the protector of such places, and it is believed that the white-walled town **church of Kassiopitissa** now occupies the site of a Temple of Jupiter, once visited by the Emperor Nero. On one of Kassiópi's headlands lie the ruins of a 13th-century castle.

The beaches nearby are pebbly and involve a short walk over the headlands; the ones nearest the town offer a good range of **watersports,** with boats for hire. The town is just over an hour by bus from Corfu Town, with four buses daily in summer. The resort's appeal is mainly to younger holidaymakers, as the lack of an easy-to-reach beach discourages families; at the height of the season the fishermen will probably be back from their night's work before the bars in the centre have closed their doors behind the last customers.

Andinióti Lagoon ★★

At the northern tip of Corfu lies this lagoon, surrounded by reed-beds and a haven for **wildlife**. Several varieties of heron can be seen fishing here, the reeds hide warblers, and terrapins swim beneath the waves. Marsh harriers and nightingales are other residents. A church and a single taverna mark the sandy beach of **Áyios Spiridhon**. The headland here is a delightful place to explore: from the main beach a rough track leads off to the right to a quieter beach; to the left is the channel connecting the Andinióti Lagoon with the sea. By crossing the bridge over this channel you come to another headland, more

MOSQUITOES

Corfu is a hot and lush island with several lagoons – ideal mosquito territory. There are no malarial mosquitoes, so you won't require inoculations, but you may need some personal protection from mosquito attack, particularly in the evening and at night. A little insect repellent on wrists and ankles when going out in the evening can help. The most effective deterrent in your bedroom is the plug-in device which slowly burns a small blue tablet overnight. Widely available all over Corfu, these are very effective.

remote and usually crowd-free, ideal for not-too-strenuous walking and fertile territory for naturalists.

Akharávi and Ródha ★★★

These two resorts stand close to each other on an unbroken stretch of **golden sand** extending for 8 kilometres (5 miles). Despite the growing popularity of the resorts, it is always possible to find a quiet, private spot on a beach of that size, and the sand shelves very gently in places, making ideal bathing conditions for young children. The original village of **Akharávi** is a few hundred metres inland, and in the olive groves between it and the coast lie villas and some small hotels. You will still find fishermen here, but the village is increasingly turning to tourism. **Ródha** has already done so, with a greater number of hotels, including the large Ródha Beach Hotel. It also has the remains of a 5th-century BC Doric temple, although most visitors will be more interested in the car and bike hire, tavernas, bars and watersports offered by both these pleasant but rather characterless resorts. Boat trips are available; regular destinations include Corfu Town, nearby resorts like Sidhari and Kassiópi, and, further afield, Paleokastrítsa and the off-shore islands.

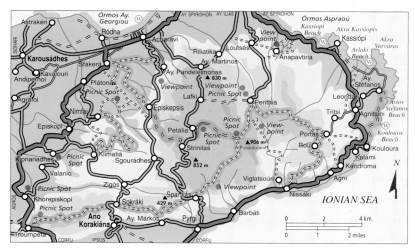

The Northeast at a Glance

BEST TIMES TO VISIT

April/May to see orchids and other flowers if you're planning to walk on Mount Pandokrator; **July** and **August** for fun and sun; or **May/June** and **September** for a quieter holiday . . . but still with sun.

GETTING THERE

The resorts closest to Corfu Town are easily reached by **taxi**, and all can be reached by a good **bus service** which runs along the coast road. Some buses leave from the New Fortress bus station on Amraviou, the main street on the far side of the New Fortress from the port. One service goes to Ipsos/Pyrgi and another to Nissáki and Kalámi. A service to Kondókali, Gouvía and Dassia leaves from San Rocco Square (Platía Theotóki).

To get further north there is the bus which runs four times daily from Corfu Town's New Fortress bus station and goes along the coast via Nissáki and Kalámi to Áyios Stéfanos and Kassiópi. A different bus route from the same station goes inland to Akharávi and Ródha.

If you want to drive, there are plenty of car rental offices in Corfu Town, belonging to both international and local companies. Both the airport and Old Port area have a number. You can also hire mopeds or light motorcycles, but this mode of travel is not recommended because of the poor state of some minor roads and the unreliability of some of the machines rented out. There is a high accident rate.

GETTING AROUND

Buses link the major resorts and villages, and **taxis** are available for shorter journeys. Although buses and taxis are the usual means of transport, **hitch-hiking** should not be too difficult on the busy coast road. All resorts offer **excursion trips**, often by boat to a remote beach, picking you up again later in the day.
Europcar has rental offices in Akharávi, tel 0663-63843 and Ródha, tel 0663-63726. There are local car rental firms in all the resorts – even in some small places.

WHERE TO STAY

Akharávi

Akharávi Beach: pleasant small B grade hotel a short walk from the centre, with pool and tennis courts, tel 0663-93146.
Beis Beach: B grade, but larger than Akharávi Beach and with more facilities, tel 0663-63077.
Ionian Princess: B grade hotel 5 minutes' walk from the beach, with large pool (children's section), sun terrace and gardens, tel 0663-63110.
St George's Bay Club: offers good A standard rooms, but as self-catering accommodation, tel 0663-93203.

Dassia

Amalia: small C grade hotel, a litttle way from the beach, but with a good-sized swimming pool and sun terrace, tel 0661-93523.
Dassia Chandris and **Corfu Chandris**: two old established A grade hotels with every amenity where guests benefit by the sharing of facilities, tel 0661-33873 and 33871 respectively.
Paradise: B grade medium-sized hotel, in a quiet location at the top of a hill, some distance from beach and village centre, tel 0661-91438.

Gouvía

Corcyra Beach: large A grade hotel with private beach, lovely gardens and all facilities, tel 0661-30770.
Louvre: small, family-owned C grade hotel five minutes' walk from the beach; quiet and with its own taverna, tel 0661-91972.

Ipsos

Ipsos Beach: B rated, but the best in Ipsos, tel 0661-93232.
Sunrise: pleasant furnished apartments, B rated, tel 0661-93414.

Kalámi

Villa Matela: small pension with A grade facilities, tel 0663-91371.

Kassiópi

Apraos Bay Hotel: slightly out of the centre, quiet and modern but built in traditional style, tel/fax 0662-81350.
Frossyni's Gardens: A grade furnished apartments, tel 0663-81258.

The Northeast at a Glance

Poseidon: A grade furnished apartments, tel 0663-81439.
Komméno
Astir Palace: one of Corfu's handful of Luxury grade hotels. In splendid isolation on a headland, it has private beaches, pool, gardens, good views, tel 0661-91481.
Radovas: this A grade hotel, only 5 minutes from he seafront, offers plenty of facilities including pool, sun terrace, regular disco, tel 0661-91218.
Kondókali
Kondókali Bay: Luxury grade with good sports facilities, tel 0661-38736.
Nissáki
Nissáki Beach : large A grade hotel offering pools, sports, shops, disco, taverna, tel 0663-91232.
Pyrgi
Anna Liza Apartments: the only A grade accommodation in Pyrgi, tel 0661-93438.
Ródha
Ródha Beach: large B grade hotel with pools, own beach and gardens, tel 0663-93202/31225.
Ródha Inn Hotel: small C grade hotel, central, by the sea, with taverna, bar and Greek dancing, tel 0663-63358.

Agni
Taverna Nikolas: in a delightful setting on a quiet beach, but you may need to book a table and a boat to get you there, tel 0663-

91136/91243, fax 0663-91369.
Akharávi
Valentino: slightly out of the centre but recommended.
Dassia
Kiki's Fish Taverna: near the Elea Beach Hotel, serves nothing but fish – which consequently tends to be good.
Taverna Castello: family-run taverna serving traditional dishes, tel 0661-93654.
Gouvia
Restaurant Plato, towards Kondókali: serves both Greek and French cuisine, tel 0661-91358.
Ipsos
Phoebus Restaurant: English-run with a Corfiot chef and open all day.
Kalámi
Pepe's Taverna: family-run with Corfiot dishes, fresh fish and Saturday folk dancing, tel 0663-91180.
Kamináki
Spiro's Taverna: on the beach, serves Spiro's mother's home cooking, tel 0663-91211.
Kassiópi
Kassiópi Star: serves traditional Greek food popular with locals as well as visitors.
Sze Chuan: one of the few Chinese restaurants in the Greek islands, with a branch in Corfu Town as well, tel 0663-81097.
The Three Brothers: typical Greek taverna on the harbour, its atmosphere not yet spoiled by the increasing tourist trade, tel 0663-81211.

Kondókali
Takis Taverna: typical Corfiot taverna serving traditional dishes.
The Viceroy Indian Restaurant: offers a rare chance to eat from a tandoori oven in Greece.
Ródha
Ródha Inn Hotel has a good restaurant open to non-residents, tel 0663-63358.

Agathi's Lace in Kassiópi sells hand-made lace and rugs tel 0663-81315.
Danilia Village, tel 0661-91621.
Jet Ski Water Club runs watersports in Kondókali, tel 0661-91358.
Leather Workshop in Gouvía, for goods at factory prices, tel 0661-27288.
Salco Holidays Tourist Bureau in Kassiópi deals with car hire, trips, rooms and boat hire, tel 0663-81317/81437.
The Travel Corner in Kassiópi for ferries, excursions, etc, tel 0663-81220/81213, fax 0663-81108.
Travel N S K in Ródha for car hire, rooms, excursions and currency exchange, tel 0663-63471/63274, fax 0663-63274.
Traveller Ltd, Swedish-owned tour agency in Gouvía for car hire, boats, rooms, tel 0661-91008/90527, fax 0661-91868.
Waterhoppers, scuba diving centre in Ipsos, tel 0661-93867.

4
The Northwest

Paleokastrítsa has the reputation of being the most beautiful place on Corfu, and despite the crowds that such a description attracts, it is hard to disagree. Some enthusiasts go even further and call it one of Europe's most attractive spots, with its beaches, coves, woodlands, spectacular sunsets and steep winding streets.

The northwestern corner of the island has other attractions, giving you the choice of busy beach spots such as **Sidhari**, quieter resorts like **Aríllas**, or the even more get-away-from-it-all feeling provided by the **offshore islands** of Eríkoussa, Othoní and Mathráki. History buffs can muse on the island's chequered past at the ruined fortress of Angelókastro, and lovers of landscape can marvel at the sunset-lit colours along the striated cliffs of Sidhari and Pérouládhes. There are golden beaches like the one in beautifully situated **Áyiou Yióryiou** for those who want to work on nothing more strenuous than their suntan, while the more energetic will enjoy the windsurfing at **Áyios Stéfanos**, the other watersports available just about everywhere, or a round of golf over 18 holes on the southern edge of the fertile **Rópa Plain**, courtesy of Corfu's only golf club

Sidhari **

Sidhari is centered on a lovely stretch of beach, which has resulted in the development of the village into a **busy package holiday resort**. If not quite as frenetic as the places nearer to Corfu Town, such as Benitses, it still has plenty of bars to make the place buzz at night. And

Opposite: *The black robes and long beards of Greek Orthodox priests are an imposing and frequent sight all over Greece.*

FOR THE YOUNG AND SINGLE

There are several Corfu
resorts for which the word
busy is an understatement,
especially if visiting in July or
August. In the height of summer they are taken over
almost exclusively by young
people, mainly from Britain,
and mainly in search of drink,
nightlife, sex and sunshine,
not necessarily in that order.
If this is what you want, the
places to head for are
Benitses, Kávos, Ipsos, Pyrgi
and Kassiópi.

the beach is ideal for young children, with shallow
waters as well as the splendid sands.

The resort packs a lot into a small space. The one
main street runs by the beach and carries the through
traffic, but this is usually slow and light, while a parade
of shops and tavernas between the road and the beach
helps shield sunbathers from petrol fumes and noise.
There are several hotels, but all are small and most are
family-run. Other accommodation is in villas, both in the
village and hidden in the **attractive groves of trees** inland.

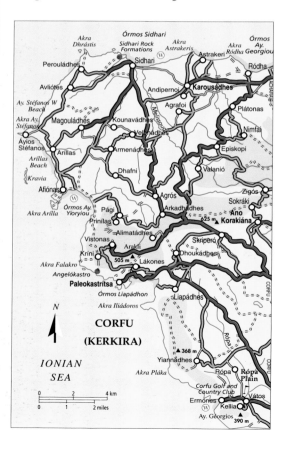

TAXIS

There is no shortage of taxis
in Corfu Town, and each
smaller town and village will
probably have a taxi or two.
In summer there may appear
to be too few to go round, as
licences are limited and the
numbers are dictated by the
needs of the local people
rather than the requirements
of summer visitors. Taxis are
cheap, and locals often use
them for long journeys.
Although cars are metered, a
fare may be negotiable for a
specific journey, with the driver agreeing to pick you up
again later in the day.

Sidhari has long been noted for its coves and **rock formations**. There are plenty of quiet coves along the coast which can be reached on foot, on a boat trip or simply by paddling your own canoe or pedalo. Any number of other boat trips are available, to resorts such as Paleokastrítsa, or to the offshore islands. There is a regular bus service to Corfu Town, and visitors can hire cars, motorcycles, bicycles, boats and even horses, to ride along the impressive, yellow sandstone cliffs or to explore the peaceful agricultural region behind Sidhari for a glimpse of everyday Corfiot life. Sidhari is one of the oldest known settlements on the island – archaeologists have unearthed the remains of a pre-Neolithic community of about 7000BC.

The Canal d'Amour in the rock formations at Sidhari.

One popular feature of the resort is the so-called **Canal d'Amour**, a channel rather than a tunnel of love. This was formed between two large rocks in the bay, where the action of the sea on the soft sandstone produced a small tunnel, which the continued erosion eventually turned into a fully-fledged channel. You can believe whichever you prefer of the several different legends about it: that any person swimming the channel while it is in shade will always be lucky in love; that any couple swimming through it, shaded or not, will stay together forever; or that any woman swimming through it will win the man of her dreams.

NUDISM

Nude sunbathing is illegal in
Greece except on the few
specially designated beaches.
The only one on Corfu is at
Mirtiótissa. Nudity is, however, tolerated if confined to
remote beaches where no
local people are likely to be
offended. Some large beaches may have an unofficial
nudist section at one end.
Topless sunbathing is now so
common on almost all popular beaches as to be accepted, but care should be taken
not to cause offence if using
family beaches near town
centres. While the Greeks are
not overly puritanical, they do
have a strong sense of decen-
cy and an offence against this
could bring a fine or even
imprisonment.

Right: *The strange rock formations at Sidhari ensure
there are several protected
coves to swim in.*
Opposite: *Water provides
entertainment – including
fishing and sailing elegant
flotilla yachts – for locals
and tourists alike.*

Pérouládhes *

About 3km (2 miles) to the west of Sidhari, in a striking
setting, are the beach and handful of houses that make
up Pérouládhes. The village is easily found by following
the main road out of Sidhari to the west, then taking the
right-hand turning, signposted for the **Sunset Taverna**.
As the name suggests, this is a popular evening spot,
with high cliffs behind a beautiful sandy beach. The cliffs
are a colourful mix of compressed clays and earth, at
their best when the rays of the setting sun hit them. In
front lies a **golden beach** of fine sand, delightful if you
are there slightly out of season, though in high summer
and especially at weekends it is rather too popular for its
small size.

If the beach is full, many people seek a little space by
walking north out of the village to explore Corfu's most
northerly point, the promontory of Cape Dhrástis. This is
composed of more cliffs surrounding small coves, with
offshore rocks and distant views of the islands of Othoní,
Mathráki and Eríkoussa.

Áyios Stéfanos **

One of the two Corfu resorts called Áyios Stéfanos (the
other is in the northeast), this is also sometimes referred
to as San Stefano. It is ideal for those looking for a quiet
holiday in a village that has not surrendered its essential

Greekness to the tourist invasion. For the present Áyios Stéfanos remains a **fishing village**, with boats rocking in the small harbour below a church at the end of a sandy bay. There are beachside tavernas and watersports available – this westernmost point of Corfu is especially good for **windsurfing**. Accommodation is in a handful of villas, private rooms and apartments, although at the time of writing the first hotel was in the process of being built.

A surprisingly good bus service connects Áyios Stéfanos, at the end of the line, with Sidhari (25 minutes) and on to Corfu Town (95 minutes) five times daily in summer. A short and enjoyable walk of less than an hour over the wooded headland brings you to the next resort to the south, Aríllas.

Aríllas *

Aríllas is another of the **relatively quiet** resorts in the northwest corner of Corfu, less accessible than other parts of the island though even Aríllas clings on to its connection with the capital via a twice-daily bus service that takes almost two hours through the inland mountain villages. The journey provides an opportunity to glimpse a little 'real' Corfiot life in these remote settlements, where the pace slows down to that of a donkey and there isn't a disco in sight. As in Áyios Stéfanos, the winds here on the western extremity of Corfu makes Aríllas popular with windsurfers, and boards, boats and pedaloes can all be hired. The beach is mostly sand with some shingle, and runs for about a kilometre around the bay. There are three small C class hotels, a few bars and tavernas, and a solitary disco.

TRULY RURAL

The villages in the hills behind the coastal resorts are worth taking the trouble to visit. They offer an opportunity to observe typical Corfiot rural life, unaffected by tourism – to the extent that, though most have a café, you can't bank on getting a meal. Even if you don't have a car, some of the buses to Corfu Town go through the villages, and a careful study of the timetables should enable you to spend a few hours exploring the villages and the mountains around.

The Offshore Islands ★★★

From many points along the northwest coast you can see three small islands, all of which can be visited from Sidhari or on the twice-weekly official ferry from Corfu Town. Day-trips are also possible in high season from other resorts including Kassiópi and Áyios Stéfanos. The day-trippers seldom venture further than the nearest beach, so even in high season the islands are probably the best chance you have in Corfu of **getting away from it all**. Facilities are limited, so if you plan to stay you need to make sure accommodation is available before you go.

The most popular of the three is **Eríkoussa**, which has one small hotel and rooms to rent in the main village. This village – Eríkoussa – boasts a glorious sandy beach, and there are others on the island, none more than a short walk away through the heather or the cypress groves. There are two more small villages inland, though neither of these has a taverna, the only one being in Eríkoussa itself (on the beach), where you will also find a few shops and cafés.

To the west of Eríkoussa is **Othoní**, the largest of the islands, which has slightly more by way of facilities but – with just a few mainly shingle stretches – lacks the attractive beaches of Eríkoussa. The island offers good anchorage for visiting yachts, and there are several tavernas, shops, cafés and rooms to rent. A single road leads from the harbour to the solitary inland village, through quiet olive groves and pine woods, to the other side of the island and a few more remote but rocky beaches. There is also a well preserved medieval fort on one of the island's hilltops. Othoní has been identified with the island home of Calypso, the nymph who kept Odysseus captive for seven years in Homer's *Odyssey*; boat trips can be made to 'Calypso's cave'.

Southeast of Othoní is **Mathráki**, the smallest of the trio, with two tiny villages joined by a strip of road, a single taverna and just a few rooms to rent. The long sandy beach on the east coast is a nesting site for the rare loggerhead turtle, so camping here is forbidden. Though small, the island is green and appealing.

Áyiou Yióryiou ★★★

It would be hard to better the setting for this small but growing resort, with its sandy bay guarded by two headlands and backed by green mountain slopes. The **excellent beach** runs for 3km (2 miles) and offers good windsurfing, with water-skiing and jet-skiing also available. The sheer size of the beach, the fact that part of it is not accessible by road, and the availability of other beaches nearby all mean that the resort has not yet been swamped by its increasing popularity. However, more small hotels are being built and there is no lack of bars and restaurants, so Áyiou Yióryiou, delightfully situated as it is, may soon be transformed into a bustling beach playground. Meanwhile, for a magnificent view – a vast panorama back over the bay and the headland beyond – walk up the rough road towards the lovely hill village of **Pági** (by which name the beach is also sometimes known), and through the tall cypress trees.

There are several resorts that bear the name of Áyiou Yióryiou, St George, but this one in the northwest is one of the least spoilt.

Angelókastro **

Between Pági and Paleokastrítsa lies the village of **Makrádes**, and from here a path leads towards the headland on which stand the ruins of the 13th-century fortress of Angelókastro – the climb takes about 20 minutes. The fortress is named after **Michael II Angelos Komnenos**, who as Despot of Epirus ruled Corfu in the 13th century and is believed to have finished the building of the fortress, although its precise history is uncertain. It is believed that its original purpose was as a defence against Genoese pirates. One thing that is known is that during the Turkish invasion of 1571, people from the surrounding villages sought safety in the castle. When the main strength of the Turkish attack had gone, the villagers emerged to drive the remaining invaders off. The Turks sailed away to defeat at the hands of Christian forces in the Battle of Lepanto in the Gulf of Corinth.

From this impregnable spot – the fortress was never taken – there are marvellous **views** south to Paleokastrítsa and, when the weather is clear, even across the island to the Old Fortress in Corfu Town: the two fortresses used to warn each other of impending attacks. There is not much left of Angelókastro, apart from a few walls and a well preserved cistern. Nearby are some hermit cells and caves (one housing a shrine) and, on the hill's highest point, a chapel dedicated to the Archangels Michael and Gabriel.

Paleokastrítsa ***

This is both the most popular and most attractive resort on Corfu's west coast. Many regard it as the most beautiful spot on the whole island, and one of the first to fall for its charms was **Sir Frederick Adam**, British High Commissioner to the Ionian Islands in the early 19th century. Its appeal then lay in its steep wooded slopes, blue sea and several lovely bays with bathing beaches. One problem was its comparative inaccessibility, so Sir Frederick had a road built to the village, with the ostensible purpose of erecting a military convalescent home

Dance displays like this may be put on for the benefit of visitors, but they still form a part of modern Greek life, with some very skilful practitioners.

there. This was never built, but Sir Frederick now found it much easier to take his regular picnics in Paleokastrítsa. Such illustrious travellers as Empress Elizabeth of Austria, Kaiser Wilhelm of Germany and the English writer and artist Edward Lear soon followed in his footsteps.

Today there are fewer trees and many more buildings, but the setting has lost none of its beauty. Paleokastrítsa is more of a **family resort** than many on Corfu, as the swimming is safe in any of its three main coves – Áyia Triada, Platakia and Alipa – and off other minor beaches around, although the waters here are notably cold. The beaches are a mix of sand, pebble and shingle, most of them served by a taverna and other facilities – boat trips, water-skiing, canoes and a diving school – in summer. From the harbour you can take boat trips along the coast to look at the many grottoes in the vicinity, and out around the Rock of Kolovri, which –

GREEK DANCING

It is the unlucky visitor who will not see at least one example of Greek dancing on a visit, whether staged or spontaneous. It is one of the oldest of Greek art forms, and shows no signs of dying out. Greek dances can be either *syrtós* (shuffling) or *pidiktós* (leaping), both being performed in a circular manner, though the circle is not always evident when the number of dancers is small. Some series of movements can be very complicated, but the visitor who tries to follow them will be heartily applauded. Greeks need little encouragement to dance.

like Mouse Island off Kanóni – is said to be the petrified ship of Odysseus. The palace of Alcinous, king of the Phaeacians and father of Nausicaa who discovered Odysseus after his shipwreck, is reputed to have stood nearby. According to another legend, the Rock of Kolovri is the ship of an Algerian pirate intent on looting the monastery on the headland (see page 89). As the ship approached the shore, it was turned to stone in answer to the prayers of the Abbot. Today the rock is the haunt of seabirds.

The town itself now has well over a dozen hotels to choose from, plus villas and rooms to rent. Anyone who is not fully fit should note that the streets are very steep. There is no lack of bars and tavernas and, while it does not attract young single holidaymakers, Paleokastrítsa's popularity makes it not a place to choose if your aim is to get away from it all. That having been said, there are quieter beaches a short walk away, and the town's spectacular location does make it a good base for walkers.

Theotokos Monastery ★★

One of Paleokastrítsa's headlands is the high perch of the Theotokos Monastery, also known as the Monastery of Panayias Paleokastrítsas. A good time to visit is towards **sunset**, when most day-trippers have left and the sea and bays are aglow with the last of the golden-pink light: the monastery stays open until 20:00 from April to October. The first monastery on this site is thought to have been built in 1228, but the present buildings date from the 17th and 18th centuries. It is thought that in the Middle Ages the monastery was linked to the fortress of Angelókastro on the steep hill behind (see page 86). A monk often greets visitors with a glass of cold water drawn straight from the well, although the

DRESS SENSE

Most monasteries and convents will refuse admission to visitors who are not respectfully dressed. This can come as a surprise to those who are used to the casual approach to dress that is the norm on Corfu. But these are holy places, and it causes offence if visitors arrive in little more than brief swimsuits. Men should wear long trousers and women should wear skirts and avoid bare shoulders, although in some places shorts may be acceptable. It is better to be cautious and wear (or carry) suitable clothing, than to travel some distance to see a religious building and be unable to enter. If in doubt make enquiries before setting out.

Admission to monasteries like this one at Paleokastrítsa is usually free, but a small donation, made perhaps by buying and lighting a candle, will be appreciated to help pay for the upkeep.

monastery is no longer active and the monks' cells are empty. There is a flagged courtyard, lemon trees and an atmosphere of tranquillity. The **church** has an unusual painted and carved ceiling and a fine collection of icons. There is also a small **museum** with an eclectic display of shells, bones, icons and old books, an old olive press and large gardens where you can escape the heat of the sun.

Lákones **

Lákones is visited chiefly for its **superb views** over Paleokastrítsa, but is itself an attractive hillside village clinging to the slopes of Mount Arakli, Corfu's third highest peak at 405m (1330ft). It has one narrow main street, through which a steady string of tour buses pass bearing day-trippers to its more famous neighbour. There are any number of tavernas, each allegedly offering the best views in the village – and priced accordingly. In fact the best view is outside Lákones at the Bella Vista café. This delightful if busy spot has a view perhaps only rivalled by the sight of Vlachérna and Pondikoníssi at Kanóni. Lákones makes an excellent base for those who enjoy **walking**. There are rooms to rent in the village, and a choice of excellent walks.

The Rópa Plain *

South of Paleokastrítsa is a long undeveloped stretch of coast, inaccessible by road because of a range of hills, although boat trips will take sunbathers to some of its beaches. The next major resort, Ermónes (see page 94), is about 10km (6 miles) south, the gap being filled inland by the flat and fertile Rópa Plain, a region of corn fields, vines, fruit and vegetable production and dairy farming. This was once marshland noxious with malaria-carrying mosquitoes until the occupying Italians drained it some 50 years ago. The plain is watered by the River Rópa, and its lushness is such that it is the site of the Corfu Golf and Country Club with Corfu's only **golf course**. The clubhouse features a bar and restaurant open to non-members, and horse riding is also available at the Rópa Valley Riding Stables based here.

GOLF

Corfu is proud of its golf course in the Rópa Valley, which is of international standard and attracts regular golfers from Athens and the rest of Europe. One member flies over regularly from Ioánnina on the mainland and goes back again the same day, after one round of golf. There is increasing interest in the sport in Greece, with the Government and NTOG putting funds into the building of new courses and the development of existing ones. The Corfu Golf Club already offers a 6218m (6800yd) course, with putting green, practice ground and lessons from a professional.

The Northwest at a Glance

Midsummer if you like it busy, **May/June** or **September** for more peace and space.

A good **bus service** from the New Fortress Square station links Corfu Town with Paleokastrítsa, while another service runs from the same station to Sidhari, Pérouládhes and Áyios Stéfanos.

Apart from the bus service, use **taxis** for short hops and **excursions/boats** to visit other resorts. Regular boats visit the offshore islands.

Aríllas
Aríllas Beach is a smallish C class hotel, tel 0663-31401.
Hotel Belle Helene is a clean but simple beachside hotel, with taverna and pool attached, tel 0663-96201.

Áyiou Yióryiou
Costas Golden Beach is C class, attractively placed with a pool; most rooms overlook the beach, tel 0663-96207.

Paleokastrítsa
Akrotiri Beach is the only A class hotel in the resort, with its own pool, bars, disco and games, tel 0663-41275.
Oceanis is a medium-sized B class hotel with pool, restaurant and Greek music and dancing, tel 0663-41229.
Paleokastrítsa is a large B class hotel with pool, children's

playground, restaurant and nightclub, tel 0663-41207.

Sidhari
Mimosa, close to the beach, is C class with restaurant and snack bar, tel 0663-95363, fax 0663-95361.
Sidhari Beach is C class, on a beach away from the town centre with restaurant and basic facilities, tel 0663-95215.

Áyiou Yióryiou
Delfini: has a delightful terrace and offers fresh local fish and lobster, tel 0663-41378.
Taverna Afionis: good honest Greek taverna at the north end of the beach.

Lákones
Bella Vista: on the edge of the village, offering unrivalled views and plain Corfiot cooking.

Paleokastrítsa
Chez George: right on the beach and priced accordingly, but offering reasonable food, tel 0663-41233.

Pérouládhes
Sunset, on the Sidhari road: specializes in oven-cooked and spit-roast dishes, tel 0663-95334.

Rópa Plain
Livadi Country Club: offers Greek, English and French cooking, with an emphasis on game, tel 0661-94929.

Sidhari
Oasis: generally considered the resort's best restaurant, though out of the centre. Boat trips to the offshore islands are popular.

Mike's Water Sports at Paleokastrítsa books excursions and rents out watersports facilities, tel 0663-41510, fax 0663-41486.
Sidhari Tourist Services arranges car hire, cruises and other excursions, tel 0663-95257, fax 0663-95066.
Sidhari Travel can deal with most tourist needs in most languages, tel 0663-95375/95155/95055, fax 0663-95343.
Vlasseros Travel offers excursions, rooms, car hire and horse riding through the **Vlasseros Horse Riding Club**, tel 0663-95062/95655, fax 0663-95695.

Automobile Club arranges car hire in Sidhari, tel 0663-95027/95345.
Baracuda Club in Paleokastritsa gives scuba diving lessons, tel 0663-41211.
Corfu Golf Club is an 18-hole, 72-par championship course, tel 0661-94220.
Costas Cars and Bikes at Áyiou Yióryiou, tel 0663-96298.
Jim's Bikes in Sidhari specializes in motorcycles and mopeds, tel 0663-95345.
Kostas Kantarelis in Sidhari books rooms, excursions and deals with most tourist needs, tel 0663-95314.
Rópa Valley Riding Stables based at the Golf and Country Club offers hires for beginners or experienced riders, tel 0661-94220.

5
The Centre and South

The eastern and western coastlines of the centre – Corfu's slim waist – could hardly be more different in the way they have developed. The east coast has a straight stretch of good road which runs for about 10km (6 miles) to the south of Corfu Town, and is lined by lively resorts not as close together as their counterparts on the coast to the north of the capital, but just as popular. In **Benitses** the south can boast *the* ultimate brash package holiday centre. Questionable taste of a different sort is displayed nearby in the bizarre palace of Elizabeth of Austria, the **Achillíon**. The road finally turns inland as it reaches the smaller villages of **Moraitika** and **Messongi**.

The cliff-lined central west coast has no such convenient road – going from one resort to the next often involves a round-about journey – so that between tourist resorts like **Ermónes** and **Glifadha** you will find quiet coves, accessible only on foot or by boat, and some of the best sandy beaches on the island.

Corfu's southern extremity has only one resort, **Kávos**, for those who like things wild and loud at night. Otherwise the beach resorts are small and well separated, like **Áyios Yióryios**, good for beach-lovers, and **Petriti**, little more than a fishing village with a bit of tourism. The main road runs down the centre of this narrowing strip, seldom far from a turning that leads down to a beach, often deserted. There are many inland farming villages to explore, plus **Lake Korission** (Límni Koríssia), a peaceful haven for wildlife. At the southern tip are the white sand beaches of Cape Asprókavos.

Don't Miss

*** Mirtiótissa: one of the island's best beaches
*** The Achillion: bizarre, but unique
*** Lake Korission: good beaches and wildlife areas
** Benites: the archetypal sun'n'fun tourist resort
** Pélekas: attractive hill town, with Kaiser's Throne
** Sinarádhes Folk Museum: the only one on Corfu.
** Kávos: a raucous resort
** Petrití: pleasant, not over-developed fishing village.

Spilio is typical of Corfu's mountain villages, hardly touched by tourism.

HITCH-HIKING

Hitch-hiking is legal in Corfu, and lifts should not be too hard to come by as Greek drivers are generally helpful. However, cars and vans are frequently full of friends and relatives being transported here and there; also as the basic Greek motor insurance policy does not cover accidents to passengers many otherwise willing drivers will not take the risk of a potentially costly accident. But patience should pay off, even if your lift is in the back of a bumping van on a bag of watermelons, with sheep as your fellow travellers.

OFF THE BEATEN TRACK

Corfu is a good place for walking, as it normally misses the extreme midsummer heatwaves that frequently strike Athens and the Aegean Islands. However, walkers should always be prepared for the chance of rain and be aware that mists can come down without warning on the higher slopes of the hills. On the whole, the holiday-makers attracted to Corfu want to do little more than lie on a beach during the day; as a result those few foreign visitors who take the trouble to visit the more remote villages are treated all the more hospitably by the villagers.

THE CENTRE
Ermónes *

On the edge of the Rópa Plain and a convenient base if you want to combine time on the beach with trips to the nearby **golf course** (see page 90), Ermónes is a busy little resort, its bay overlooked by the bungalows of the Ermónes Beach Hotel. The beach is a mix of sand, shingle and larger rocks, and in summer there seem to be as many people in the water as there are pebbles on the shore. Facilities include water-skiing, canoeing, pedaloes, paragliding, boat hire, boat trips and scuba diving. If watersports and golf are not enough, there are four tennis courts open to the public at the Ermónes Beach Hotel, which is reached by funicular from the back of the beach. This is not an ideal place for children: apart from the frantic watersports and the shingle surface, the beach shelves quite sharply.

Ermónes boasts two **legends** (suspiciously similar to those recounted in Paleokastrítsa up the coast, see page 88). The largest of the rocks in the bay is said to be a

pirate chief who was turned to stone for attempting to
steal an icon from the church; some prefer to see it as a
petrified nun. It is also claimed that it was here, where
the Rópa river reaches the sea, that Odysseus was
washed ashore naked in the *Odyssey*. Homer's hero had
just escaped from the amorous nymph Calypso (whose
home is said to have been on the offshore island of
Othoní) when Poseidon turned his ship to stone. He
reached the beach to be found by Nausicaa, the
Phaeacian king's daughter, who had been washing some
clothes in a nearby spring with her handmaidens.
Ermónes does have a convenient freshwater spring, and
other evidence suggests that Homer may well have had
Ermónes in mind as the setting for this part of his epic
tale – sufficient for one of the tavernas here to have
named itself the Nausicaa. There are a number of other
places to get food and drink plus two hotels.

*Ermónes has its Homeric
connections, though most
people are happy just to lie
on its beach.*

Opposite: *Flotilla sailing is popular in the Ionian Sea, allowing holiday-makers the freedom to tie up at appealing small harbours.*

Vátos *

A popular walk for people based at Ermónes is the 2km (1¹/₄ miles) to the inland village of Vátos, which has a small hotel, a few shops and two tavernas. There is also a campsite situated about a kilometre outside the village, also called Vátos. Cut off from the coast by the 392m (1286ft) slopes of **Mount Áyios Yióryios**, is an attractive place to visit with its with small whitewashed houses, and provides a peaceful contrast to the busy beaches. Follow the path up from the village for a great view over the plain and the coast.

SAILING IN AND AROUND CORFU

Yachts entering Greek waters must fly the 'Q' flag till cleared by one of the official entry posts which are listed below. On first arrival, you will be given a transit log, which is obligatory. After clearance, it is customary to fly a Greek courtesy flag. Weather warnings are given in English by the Greek Meteorological Service over the radio telephone service every 30 minutes (tel [01] 894-0616). For more detailed information obtain a current copy of the booklet *Greece for the Yachtsman*, issued by the NTOG and updated from time to time. Contact the NTOG office in your own country for a list of local yacht chartering companies.

BEST TIMES FOR SAILING
The waters around Corfu are particularly attractive to yachtsmen, with few of the still days that occur in the Aegean, and generally a pleasant light breeze. In summer watch out for the *maestros*, Corfu's equivalent of the *meltemi*, which can blow strongly from the northwest in the afternoons during July and August.

May and June usually see westerly breezes, while the prevailing wind for the rest of the year is from the southeast. The average summer wind speeds are 2.3 in September, 2.6 in April, May, August and October and 2.9 in June and July. Be prepared for wet weather at any time of year.

PORTS OF ENTRY
Cephalonia: Argostóli
Corfu: Corfu Town, Dassia, Gouvía
Ithaca: Váthi
Zákinthos: Zákinthos Town

YACHT SUPPLY STATIONS
Cephalonia: Argostóli
Corfu: Corfu Town, Gouvía, Paleokastrítsa, Kondókali
Ithaca: Váthi
Lefkas: Lefkas Town
Zákinthos: Zákinthos Town

CHARTERING BOATS IN GREECE
Ghiolman Yachts, Travel and Aviation, Filellinon 7, Athens 10557, tel (01) 323-0330, fax (01) 322-3251.
Greek Yacht Brokers and Consultants Association, PO Box 30393, Athens 10033, tel (01) 981-6582.

USEFUL CONTACTS
Athens
Hellenic Yachting Federation, Akti Navarkhou Koundourioti 4, Piraeus 18534, tel (01) 413-7351.
Sailing Federation, Xenofondos 15a, Athens, tel (01) 323-5560.
Cephalonia
Port Authorities, at Argostóli, tel 0671-22224, at Sámi, tel 0674-22031, and Póros, tel 0674-72460.
Corfu
Corfu Town Port Authority, tel 0661-32655.
Igoumenitsa
Port Authority, tel 0665-22235.
Ithaca
Port Authority, tel 0674-32909.
Killini
Port Authority, tel 0623-92211
Lefkas
Port Authority, tel 0645-22322.
Paxos
Port Authority, tel 0662-31259.
Zákinthos
Port Authority, tel 0695-22417.

Mirtiótissa ★★★

'During the afternoon . . . I slip down to the house of the peasant family and borrow the Count's placid little mare, which will take me through the vineyards and woods to what is perhaps the loveliest beach in the world. Its name is Myrtiotissa.' So wrote Lawrence Durrell in *Prospero's Cell*, and the beach is undoubtedly beautiful, with the cliffs dropping sheer to the 'lion-gold' sand and the rocks ('pitted and perforated . . . full of sea-water and winking fishes') adding a touch of drama to the remote setting. It was difficult to get to in Durrell's day, but the track has since been greatly improved and now a road zigzags down from near Vátos, signposted for the Monastery of Mirtiótissa (Our Lady of the Myrtles) from which the beach takes its name.

Inappropriately for somewhere so named, the southern section is now a **nudist beach**. The nearby **monastery** (closed 13:00–17:00) retains a secluded dignity in the midst of a grove of cypress, olive and banana trees. It was originally built in the 14th century when a monk is said to have found an icon of the Virgin Mary in one of the myrtle bushes here, but the present buildings are more recent.

The beach itself is only a narrow stretch of sand and there are no facilities other than a few snack bars. Despite this, and the relative difficulty of access, it is becoming increasingly popular and can be very crowded. There is a taverna with some rooms to rent part-way along the road down to Mirtiótissa. While it is possible to drive the whole way down to the beach since the road was improved, it is steep and not a little nerve-racking; you may prefer to walk the final stretch.

BEST BEACHES

★★★ Mirtiótissa: the loveliest beach in the world? Perhaps not that, but certainly pretty
★★★ Lake Korission: many kilometres of golden sand dunes and wildlife
★★ Áyios Gordis: headlands, hills, olive groves and several sandy stretches
★★ Glifadha: 2 kilometres of sand and a handful of tavernas on an excellent beach
★★ Santa Barbara: golden sand, and not too crowded

Not all Corfu's beaches are sandy, but this one at Glifadha has rather more than its share.

Glifadha **

This very attractive 2km (1 mile) stretch of sandy beach is reached by a steep, winding road that cuts its way through the cliffs. Glifadha is not so much a resort as a beach that has sprouted facilities, and a recent improvement in the road can only continue the development. As in a number of other resorts along Corfu's west coast, Glifadha presently functions in the shadow of one dominant hotel, in this case the Grand Hotel Glyfada Beach. Many of the visitors at the moment are day-trippers, and the area is surprisingly quiet in the evenings, with just a handful of tavernas; most people staying nearby eat in one of the two modern hotels. But during the day the beach is in full swing, with every watersport yet invented and with slightly more space on its **broad golden sands** than on the nearby narrower beach of Mirtiótissa. Bathers should take care, as there are known to be strong undercurrents just off the shore here. The beach shelves quite deeply in places, so parents should check for safety before allowing children into the water.

Pélekas **

Pélekas is one of the few villages behind the coast where tourism has taken off. It is an attractive place, its houses descending in tiers down the wooded hillside, and is famous for the superb **sunset views** over the bay below (where there is a quiet beach, popular with nudists and reached by way of a tricky path down). Pélekas was a favourite place of Kaiser Wilhelm at the turn of the century, when he spent his days at the Achillíon Palace. He came over here in the evenings to a spot now known as the **Kaiser's Throne**, an olive-shaded viewpoint at the top of the hill above the town. One of the features that appealed to him was that, at the right time of year, the setting sun can appear to slide down a hillside and into the sea. The views also take in the peak of Mount Pandokrator to the north, as well as both the west and east coasts, including Corfu Town. In Pélekas itself there are small hotels and rooms to rent, bars, shops, tavernas and tourist information offices with car hire available. The village is convenient for the exceptionally good local beaches.

Áyios Gordis ★★

This is yet another of Corfu's marvellous, long, west coast beaches, enclosed by headlands, backed by green hills and rather dominated by a large hotel on the bay. Áyios Gordis (there are several variations on its name, including Áyios Ghórdios or Áyios Górdhios) is a beach

KAISER BILL

William II (1859–1941) – full name Friedrich Wilhelm Viktor Albert – was Emperor of Germany and King of Prussia from 1888 until 1918. His confused foreign policy (he befriended then offended both Britain and Russia) contributed to the outbreak of World War I, during which he became more of a figurehead than a ruler and was a figure of fun to the British. In 1918 he left Germany for Holland, and lived there in seclusion in Doorn Castle. On his death in 1941, he was buried with full military honours by the personal order of Adolf Hitler.

Sunset over Áyios Gordis – this is often the most peaceful time of day.

In the interior, quiet roads demand exploration, preferably on foot or by bicycle.

first and a resort second; quiet in past years, it is now starting to develop, and visitors will find villas going up in the olive groves behind the beach as well as a large **Diving Centre** very evident actually on the beach. Other watersports are available too, and while the beach is a mix of sand and shingle, it shelves gently and therefore appeals to those with young children. There are tavernas and shops nearby, and in summer four buses daily make the 40-minute journey to Corfu Town, via Sinarádhes.

Sinarádhes *

In this sizable hill village between Pélekas and Áyios Gordis, two of the traditional houses have been turned into a **Folk Museum** (with unpredictable opening hours). It depicts life in a typical 19th-century home, with domestic and agricultural items and a few explanations in German and English. The museum is very low-key, and the more appealing because of it. The village itself is attractive, with flower-bedecked houses and steep, narrow streets.

North of Sinarádhes is the small, isolated coastal resort of Yialiskari, with a steeply shelving pebbly beach and dominated by the huge Yialiskari Palace Hotel.

Gardiki *

Gardiki, 10km (6 miles) south of Sinarádhes, is of greater interest as a historical site than as a tourist attraction – there is little enough to see today. Yet archaeological finds here have been dated to the Palaeolithic period (about 40,000BC), making it possibly the **oldest settlement** in the Ionian islands. In the comparatively recent 13th century AD, Michael Angelos Komnenos II – the same

Not all hotels are high-rise concrete blocks. Some are built bungalow-style, like the one at Kapodistrias pictured here near Moraitika.

Despot of Epirus who was responsible for the Angelókastro near Paleokastrítsa – built a **fortress** here. There are several higher hills in the area that he might have chosen as more defensible sites, but Gardiki's position was possibly dictated by freshwater springs. Today the fortress lies abandoned and overgrown, but its octagonal outer walls and towers retain their original height.

Not far away is the forest-girt hill village of Áyios Mattheos, clinging to the slopes of the mountain from which it takes its name. The summit is crowned by the Pandokrator Monastery, near which is a cave said to have an underground passage leading to the sea far below.

Messongi ★★

On the east coast, at the point where the busy coastal road turns inland and crosses the Messongi river, there is a sprawl of tourist development in and around the stretch of about 1km (2/3 mile) which separates Messongi from Moraitika. Messongi, where you can still sit in the old village square, has managed to cling on to its original **village atmosphere**, despite the presence nearby of large hotels and a campsite, the construction of villas and the busy nature of the rather ordinary sand and shingle beach. The **waterfront tavernas** are appealing, perfectly situated for patrons to enjoy their mainly fresh fish menus.

ESCAPES

No matter how busy the resort, it is usually quite easy to escape the crowds. The vast majority of visitors simply want to spend all day on the nearest beach, so beaches that require a small walk to reach them are often much less busy. Alternatively, head inland. That is certainly the best way of escaping the crowds at Benitses: a walk to the mountain village of **Stavrós** will enable you to survey from a position of superiority the baking flesh on the crowded beaches below. Elsewhere, hire a bike and head for the hills.

FISH

Fish is on many Greek menus, even if a lot of it will be frozen and imported. Among the fish readily found in local waters are red mullet (*barbouni*), sea bream (*sinagrida or fangri*), sole (*glossa*) whitebait (*marides*) and bass (*lithrinia*). If you like fish it is worth mugging up on the Greek names, as taverna owners often cannot translate the words into other languages.

The river ensures that the land is well watered, as it has been for centuries: some of the many large **olive trees** in and around the village are said to have been planted up to 700 years ago, when the Venetians first came. Older still are the remains of some ancient Greek temples that have been found, such as one from the 3rd century BC on a hill behind the village. There are pleasant walks to be had by heading inland up the course of the river, and to the south along a coastal track, none of them strenuous as the landscape around here is rather flatter than elsewhere on the island. To explore further afield, there are two bus services to and from Corfu Town, almost hourly in summer.

Moraitika *

The giant **Messongi Beach Hotel** (1600 beds and growing) is actually on the edge of Moraitika, by the river, and is generally held to mark the 'border' between Messongi and Moraitika. The latter is a fairly scruffy, rambling holiday spot with no heart to it, unless it is the big hotel. There's no lack of other places to stay, including the Luxury class Miramar Beach Hotel, with at least a dozen others from Grade A to Grade E able to accommodate several hundred visitors between them.

The Messongi Beach Hotel is impossible to ignore, with its 10 bars, tavernas, private gardens and shopping centre. Some of its facilities are for residents only, but in the evening it attracts its fair share of non-residents who wine, dine and dance there. The hotel's own strip of beach and the general public beach are both narrow and with shallow waters, ideal for children if a little cramped in high season. There are all the **watersports** you could wish for – windsurfing, water-skiing, paragliding, boats, canoes, pedaloes – and no shortage of places to eat and drink ranging from genuine Greek tavernas to those catering exclusively to the many British visitors who come here. For evening entertainment there are discos and a wide range of bars. From an earlier more dignified age are the remains of a Greco-Roman villa and bath house just off the main road.

Benitses ★★

Benitses has been a holiday spot since Roman times – the remains of a bath house can be seen near the harbour square – so perhaps it is appropriate that most of its summer visitors today conduct themselves as if at a Roman orgy. This is emphatically not the place to come to on Corfu if you are looking for a quiet

time and a taste of the real Greece. The taste is more likely to be British, or even Indian or Chinese, although Greek food is also widely available in the dozens of restaurants and tavernas that cram into this **busy beach resort**.

The colourful harbour at Benitses shows that even the busiest of beach resorts have not lost their Greek look completely.

For all the place's popularity, the beaches are not brilliant and get so crowded in summer that some people resort to sunbathing on the pavements. There are several sections of beach, including a man-made sandy stretch that is popular with families; the rest are small and narrow shingle strips, much frequented by those who are active only at night for the duration of their holiday here. Note, too, that the main road runs straight through Benitses, which can create problems when going to and from the beach. If they are lacking in sand and space, the beaches try to make up for it with their facilities: nowhere is further than a short stroll from a bar or restaurant, and there is every conceivable watersport. There is also a **go-kart racing track** just outside the town.

Slightly to the north of the town centre and well signposted is the **Benitses Shell Museum**. This private collection amassed by the owner over the last 20 years now amounts to several thousand shells, which make for a fascinating display. There are also whale bones and sharks' teeth, snakes and scorpions, and many examples of fine coral in subtle shades. Visitors should note that it

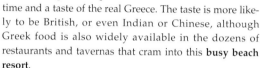

HOT FOOD

If you like your food hot, you need to take care what you order and when. Many meals are prepared at lunchtime, and simply kept warm for the evenings, which is how the Greeks like it. Stuffed tomatoes, stuffed peppers, stuffed vine leaves and moussaka are amongst the dishes best eaten at lunchtime, if you prefer to have them hot, while in the evenings you should choose something grilled, which cannot be prepared in advance.

SQUID AND OCTOPUS

Two dishes popular through-out the Mediterranean, but often less so with visitors, are squid and octopus. Fried squid (*kalamaria*) or baby squid (*kalamarakia*) are both popular starters, and deli-cious if fresh and well-cooked, while octopus (*oktapodhes*) is more often turned into a stew. Octopus meat is tenderized by hurling the creature against a hard surface, such as a rock or the harbour wall – a typical Greek sight.

is technically illegal to buy and sell coral items, because of the fast-disappearing coral reefs all round the world, but this law is commonly ignored in tourist areas. The shopkeeper might get away with selling you coral, but you could face a fine and confiscation of your purchase if it is found when you are going through customs.

Most people visit Benitses for the nightlife, not the sea-life, and here the bars and discos stay open until the last customers have gone home. Many offer laser shows, karaoke competitions and other delights – endless happy hours, non-stop film shows, draught beer – to bring people through the doors in this very competitive market.

The back streets of Benitses have their quiet spots, with the buildings regularly whitewashed around Easter time every year.

As for accommodation . . . the resort has almost 2000 beds in everything from smart A class hotels to economic E class apartments.

It is hard to believe that in among all this frenetic drinking, dancing and dating, an ordinary Greek fishing village manages to survive, but the blue and white boats in the harbour are testimony to that, as are the fishermen mending their yellow nets. Inland, too, is evidence of another Corfu, with a lush valley of olive and cypress trees, and **good walking country**. Benitses is only 12km (7½ miles) from Corfu Town, with buses almost hourly in summer taking 30 minutes to cover the journey to San Rocco Square.

Mount Áyios Dhéka **

Although Corfu's second highest peak is almost 270m (900ft) lower than Mount Pandokrator, Mount Áyios Dhéka at 576m (1889ft) still dominates this narrow stretch of central Corfu. To reach it by car from Benitses involves a long circular drive round the back of the mountain to the village of Ano Garoúna, where the road stops (cars must be left below the village itself), leaving a short walk to the summit. However, if you are reasonably fit a more direct route is to walk from Benitses, a distance of about 3km (2 miles). A track runs alongside the river and heads inland, bringing you to a minor road. If you turn left you reach the hill village of Stavrós, but a right turn along this road brings you, after about a kilometre, to a track leading off to the left that takes you to the mountain top. If you miss the path you arrive instead at the village of Áyios Dhéka, from where another track heads up to the summit with its **excellent views**.

The Achillíon has had its detractors over the years, but few could deny that it does have its elegant sections.

The Achillíon ***

Built as a palace and now a casino, it has seen service as a film set and hospital, has been called 'an abomination' and 'monstrous' – and is one of the most visited sights on Corfu. The Achillíon Palace was designed by an Italian architect and built in 1890–1 for **Empress Elizabeth of Austria** in a kitsch style that few people

One statue of Achilles was erected not by Elizabeth but by her successor at the Achillíon, Kaiser Wilhelm.

other than herself have ever appreciated. She saw it as a retreat from her personal and political problems at the Hapsburg Court, and it has to be said that the view from the Achillíon, which stands 150m (500ft) above the coast, is one of its best features – not least because you don't have to look at the palace itself. It has been dubbed neo-classical, neo-Pompeian, Teutonic and a re-creation of a Phaeacian palace, though Lawrence Durrell described it more bluntly as 'a monstrous building'.

One of Durrell's objections was to the ubiquitous sculptures, and it does seem as if you can scarcely turn a corner without bumping into some grand stone representation of a Greek or Roman figure. Principal of these is **Achilles**, Elizabeth's hero for whom the palace was named and who can be found in various histrionic postures around the place, including one overwhelming carving that is 8m (26ft) high. The grounds and gardens at least are delightful, a green oasis looking down on turquoise seas. It is sad that Elizabeth was unable to enjoy her retreat for long; she was assassinated in 1898 by an Italian anarchist, and nine years later the palace was sold to Kaiser Wilhelm II of Germany. The remains of the 'Kaiser's Bridge' can be seen down on the coast, built jutting out into the sea so that he could step straight off his boat on to land when visiting the palace. The Achillíon was used as a hospital during World War I and was the setting for some scenes in the James Bond film *For Your Eyes Only*, an appropriate title given the general opinion of Elizabeth's creation.

Gastoúrion, the nearest village to the Achillíon Palace, is a pleasant antidote to the blatant tourism of the coast and the palace. Tucked in the hills behind Benitses and Pérama, it has just a few small hotels and pensions. Coaches headed for the Achillíon drive through Gastoúrion, but it is otherwise untouched by tourism and is noted as a place where traditions in folk music and dancing are strongly maintained. It also claims to have the most beautiful women on the island, who wear their hair piled high up on their heads in a manner unique to the village.

Pérama *

On the opposite side of the Halikiopoulos Lagoon from Mouse Island and connected to Kanóni by a causeway, Pérama is the first major resort to the south of Corfu Town. It shares with Kanóni the problem of being very **close to the airport** with planes coming in to land over the causeway. This does not appear to have hindered Pérama's development as a holiday destination, however; perhaps visitors agree with the local guide, who – transforming the problem into an asset – declares that Pérama 'is a good place to watch the planes landing and taking off from the nearby airport'.

Pérama is a sprawling place, which has grown out from a small, once-attractive centre, where the Durrell family first lived when they arrived on Corfu. The finding of, and the nerve-racking drive to, the 'Strawberry-Pink' villa, is hilariously described in an early chapter of Gerald Durrell's *My Family and Other Animals*, an essential read for anyone interested in discovering what Pérama was like only 60 years ago. Today, hotels line the main southern coastal road. There are several beaches although they are mostly small and of shingle: the resorts on this coast cannot compete with those on the west, with their sweeping sandy bays. However, between them Pérama's beaches cover most watersports options, such as paragliding, water-skiing and the usual canoes, pedaloes and boat hire.

While there is no shortage of bars, restaurants and shopping facilities, Pérama, with just two late-night discos, cannot compete with nearby Benitses when it comes to frantic nightlife. Benitses is only 3.5km (2 miles) away, and Corfu Town itself not much further in the other direction. In summer there is an almost hourly bus service linking Pérama with Benitses and the capital. The resort's main appeal lies in the fact that it has an attractive green, wooded backdrop, a lushness which harks back to the times of *The Odyssey* for this is yet another spot with a Homeric connection, as it is claimed that the luxuriant gardens of the Phaeacian King Alcinous were to be found here.

TRADITIONAL DRESS

You are unlikely to see traditional costumes being worn today other than on special occasions and at folk dancing displays. The male costume is fairly standard, featuring black pantaloons and jacket over white shirt and long white stockings, but there are four types of female costume, each named after a different region of the island: *orous* (from the mountains) *agrou* (from the plains), *mesi* (from the centre) and *Lefkímmi* (from the Lefkímmi region). Unfortunately there is no substantial collection of costumes for visitors to see – just a few in the Sinarádhes Folk Museum.

BEST BARS

Bars change hands regularly in a busy tourist area like Corfu, so recommendations are difficult to give. Check the local monthly English-language publications such as *The Corfiot* and *Corfu Sun*, which carry advertisements as well as write-ups on what is happening. Look for 'Happy Hours' as a cheaper way of trying out a new bar and check prices before you buy.

THE SOUTH
Áyios Yióryios **

Not to be confused with the several other similarly
named villages scattered around Corfu, this Áyios
Yióryios is another **thriving beach resort**. On the west
coast, it is a multi-beach resort with a pair of wide, long,
sandy stretches either side of a rocky outcrop, and many
other beaches outside the village itself. In all, the beaches
stretch for almost 12km (7 1/2 miles), to the far end of Lake
Korission in the north and south past developing resorts
such as Áyia Várvara, generally known as Santa Barbara,
to a small cape called Megakhóros. One stretch to the
south is known as Golden Beach, narrow and shelving
steeply – and immensely popular. There are so many
beaches along this part of the coast that it should always
be possible to find space to yourself if that is your wish;
certain sections are used as unofficial nudist beaches.

As a place Áyios Yióryios has little heart and soul to
it, having been built up purely to cater to the tourist
trade; it certainly fulfils that function being noted for
good swimming and with a wealth of **watersports** –
water-skiing, diving, windsurfing, boating and so on.
There are several small hotels, though as yet no huge
ones, with much of the accommodation in apartments
and small self-catering villas. Car hire is available, and is
recommended if you want to explore more than the
beaches, as there is only one bus a day making the hour-
long trip to Corfu Town.

Santa Barbara *

Long undiscovered, though now on the map, Santa Barbara is a quieter spot than its neighbour to the west, Áyios Yióryios. At present it consists of little more than a deep golden, sandy beach with a few tavernas and good windsurfing conditions – there is no village as such. But facilities are increasing: already there are rooms to rent, a few small shops and evidence of more building work to come. This strip is also known as Maltas or Marathías, the names of two neighbouring beaches.

Lake Korission **

This large, shallow lake in southwest Corfu is not only excellent for sunbathing, with miles of sands and dunes, it also harbours a wealth of wildlife. You don't even need to be a keen walker to observe the wildlife: there is access for cars right to the edge of the lake. Many wading birds take advantage of the fresh water, which is a rarity on Corfu. You should see common waders such as sandpipers, dunlin, avocets and greenshanks, and – if you're lucky – catch a glimpse of great egrets and glossy ibis. In season the wild duck attract Greek hunters. Local wild flowers include Jersey orchids in spring and sea daffodils in autumn.

Sunset at the southern village of Áyios Yióryios, when the smell of fish grilling on charcoal starts to draw the crowds to the tavernas.

TOUCHING BEHAVIOUR

The Greeks are tactile people. Babies are cuddled, children have their hair ruffled, men often greet each other with a pat or a hug, and elderly people can be seen walking hand in hand with their grandchildren in the street. Young girls hold hands, and male friends may walk arm in arm. While this is normally restricted to friends and relatives, visitors may also be subject to such touches, which is a natural part of Greek behaviour. Women on their own, of course, need to keep alert and be watchful for the point where friendly touching may start to turn into unwelcome physical attention.

Petriti ★★

Petriti is the largest of a clutch of villages clustered together along a stretch of the east coast on Lefkímmi Bay. They have some tourist facilities but are in no way developed to the extent of Kávos and Áyios Yióryios. In Petriti you are likely to be searching for something to do in the evening rather than being spoilt for choice. There are three tavernas, one bar, a few shops and no beach facilities. In fact the beach here is just a small stretch of pebbles, but you will find no shortage of sandy beaches if you take a short walk either north or south. There are no hotels but several places offer rooms to rent. **Boukári**, a similar but even tinier village around the headland to the north of Petriti, has two small 20-room hotels. Either Petriti or Boukári will appeal to anyone who wishes to have a peaceful holiday in a traditional fishing village.

Kávos ★★

It seems incongruous to find Kávos right at the southern end of Corfu, literally the last resort before Cape Asprókavos, the island's southernmost point, marked by a derelict monastery. With quiet bays, fishing villages and agricultural settlements all around, suddenly Kávos

Kávos is quite a large community in the sparsely populated south, with most people to be found on its justifiably popular beach.

While most visitors worry about their tans, this Kávos fisherman makes sure his nets are ready for his next trip out to sea.

explodes like a firework. It does have one of the best beaches at this end of the island, a long stretch of sand that runs for 3km (2 miles) with a view across the Ionian Sea to the mainland. It also shelves slowly, making it ideal for young children, but any children brought here would need to be sound sleepers, for Kávos is the kind of place where the **bars and discos** stay open until the sun comes up or their customers fall down. There are said to be over 100 bars and clubs here and, though not quite so many restaurants, certainly no shortage of choice, with good seafood restaurants on the waterfront.

Every beach facility and watersport has been thought of: you can have sunbeds, umbrellas, canoes, pedaloes, water-skiing, paragliding and windsurfing, and boat trips south to the island of Paxos or north along the coast to Corfu Town. The bus to the capital takes almost two hours, but there is a good regular service – and it is one of the few which runs until quite late (for Corfu), with the last bus back leaving Corfu Town at 19:30. There are no really large hotels, most of the accommodation being in villas and blocks of self-catering apartments which are pre-booked for the season by the many tour companies, mostly British, which sell packaged holidays to Kávos.

SWEET HARMONIES

In addition to brass bands and more traditional Greek music, Corfu has a long tradition of classical music too, with no less than 15 orchestras on the island. The Philharmonic Society was formed in 1840 by the Corfiot musician, Nikolaos Mantzaros, who subsequently provided the music for the Greek national anthem. The Olympic Anthem was also composed by a member of the society, and performed by its orchestra at the first modern Olympic Games in Athens in 1896.

Central and South Corfu at a Glance

In **midsummer** – if you like it hot and busy – the main resorts are at their peak then; in **spring** or **autumn** for peace and warm weather. If you're keen on **folklore**, Lefkími (the south's admin-istrative centre) holds an annual folk festival and fiesta on 8 July.

There are a number of ser-vices from Corfu Town's vari-ous **bus** stations to Ermónes, Benitses, Glifadha, Messongi, Pérama and Vátos, and a good regular bus service runs from the New Fortress bus station to Kávos, via Messongi and the south's inland villages of Aryirádhes, Perivóli and Lefkími. The closer coastal resorts are easily reachable by **taxi** from the airport.

You can **rent a car** on arrival in Corfu Town – there are well known international companies such as Avis and Hertz here as well as local firms. Moped hire is not rec-ommended: many visitors have been involved in acci-dents because of poor road surfaces and unsatisfactorily maintained machines.

In addition to the bus services, the coast road makes **taxis** a quick option for the east coast resorts in central Corfu, with **boat** excursions and **hitch-hiking** being other easy alternatives. In the south, use

the frequent bus service along the solitary main road down the centre. From the road, nowhere is much more than 3km (2 miles) distant. Taxis are also a reasonable option, with **boats** from the main resorts serving some of the more remote beaches. **Car hire** is an alternative if you want to feel independent. Most resorts have car rental offices.

Áyios Gordis
Alonakia: B grade pension with 30 rooms, tel 0661-39239.
Áyios Gordis: the main A grade hotel in this resort, standing on its own at the end of the bay, with garden and sea views. Small swim-ming pool; beach is reached down a steep slope, tel 0661-53113.

Áyios Yióryios
Hotel Golden Sands: medi-um-sized, family-owned B grade hotel with its own pool, playground, bar, restaurant and nearby beach. Entertainment includes live music and barbecues, tel 0662-51225.

Benitses
Achilles: medium-sized grade B hotel well out of the centre with its own beach (pebbly), sun terraces and garden, tel 0661-92425.
Le Mirage: small apartment-style hotel in the centre of the resort but off the main road; C class, tel 0661-92026/7.

Potomaki: large hotel (grade B) in the centre of the resort, convenient for shops and bus to Corfu Town, tel 0661-30889.
Regency: grade A hotel away from the resort centre, with pool, poolside bar, children's pool, sauna, disco, tel 0661-92295.
San Stefano: large A grade hotel used by EU delegates at 1994 summit, tel 0661-36036.
Ermónes
Ermónes Beach: large A grade hotel with many facili-ties, including a funicular down to the beach. Sports on hand include tennis, gymnas-tics, archery and many water-sports, tel 0661-94241.
Athena Ermónes Golf: small C grade hotel in a secluded position located 5 minutes' walk from sandy beach, tel 0661-94236.
Glifadha
Glyfada Beach: medium-sized grade B hotel 5 minutes from the beach, tel 0661-94257.
Grand Hotel Glyfada: 465-room A grade establishment with sports, watersports, shopping, bars, restaurant and most other facilities, tel 0661-94201.
Kávos
Hotel Morfeas: C grade hotel with rooftop restaurant and music evenings, tel 0662-61300.
Roussos: small, pleasant B grade pension, tel 0662-22118.

Central and South Corfu at a Glance

San Marina: 120-bed family-run B grade beachside hotel, tel 0662-22455.
Messongi
Gemini: the best in the place, a B grade hotel on the main square, with pool and restaurant, tel 0661-55398.
Moraitika
Albatros: medium-sized grade B hotel a little way out of the resort centre and opposite a sandy beach, tel 0661-55315.
Kapodistrias: smallish grade B hotel in a pleasant hillside position some distance from the resort centre, opposite a sand and shingle beach, tel 0661-55319.
Messongi Beach Hotel: vast B grade hotel with every facility and 828 rooms spread over several buildings within large grounds, tel: 0661-38684.
Miramare Beach: luxury grade hotel with its own beach, gardens and shopping facilities, tel 0661-30226.
Three Stars: good-value grade C place, tel 0661-55263.
Pérama
Aeolos Beach: B grade hotel set above the coast road 15 minutes' walk from the resort. It has its own beach, gardens, a pool, children's playground, disco, tel 0661-33133.
Alexandros: the only A grade hotel in this sprawling resort, situated right in the centre, tel 0661-36855.
Oasis: medium-sized grade B hotel in the resort centre with its own beach and gardens, tel 0661-33120.

Pontikonissi: C grade hotel on the coast road, about 10 minutes' walk from the centre, with own small beach. Nicely designed in terraces, but suffers from aircraft noise, tel 0661-36871.

WHERE TO EAT

Benitses
Cutty Sark: specializes in steak and seafood dishes, tel 0661-92019/92318.
Flower Garden: has a Greek owner, British chef and serves Chinese, Indian or Greek food, tel 0661-92175.
Ermónes
Ermones Beach Hotel: the hotel taverna serves seafood and local dishes.
Kávos
Karavas is a popular restaurant, though there is little really to choose between the several lively eating places offering similar menus, such as **Naftis** and **Krinos**.
Messongi
Almond Tree: boasts a lovely beachside setting, with barbecues and fresh fish, tel 0661-75747.
Galini Restaurant: right on the beach with a mix of English and Greek cuisine.
Moraitika
The Valentino: unpromising setting but has a wide menu typical of such resorts covering Greek, Chinese, British and French cooking.
Pélekas
Sunset Restaurant: the place above town to emulate the Kaiser and watch the sun

go down; you pay for the privilege. In the village simple tavernas serve local dishes. Try the **Acropolis** or **Panorama**.
Pérama
The Pierotto: not surprisingly popular, as much for its view across to Mouse Island as for its Greek cuisine.
Santa Barbara
Dionysos: restaurant and bar offering a mix of Greek and Italian cooking, tel 0662-23157.
Vátos
Spiros Taverna: can be safely recommended, as the only two eating places here have the same name.

TOURS AND EXCURSIONS

Sinarádhes Travel at Áyios Gordis arranges accommodation, car and boat hire, plane and boat tickets and also has a currency exchange, tel 0661-53036/54118, fax 0661-53037.

USEFUL CONTACTS

The Achillíon, tel 0661-56210.
Benitses Shell Museum, tel 0661-55895.
Campsites: Vátos Camping, tel 0661-94393; **Sea Horse Camping** at Moraitika, tel 0661-75364.
Kávos Go Carts, tel 0662-61051.
Sinarádhes Folk Museum, tel 0661-35673.
Top Sail Club at Glifadha rents out canoes and offers paragliding and other water sports, tel 0661-94201.

6
Excursions

Corfu is well placed for venturing further afield. No matter where you are based, you will easily be able to get to other Ionian islands nearby and across to the mainland. Even if there are no direct trips from your base, few villages are so remote as not to have a bus service to Corfu Town, which opens up innumerable options. Be adventurous and you will discover peaceful worlds far removed from the sometimes frenetic beach and bar life of Corfu itself.

Paxos (Paxi) and Antipaxos (Antipaxi) ★★★

It is only 11km (7 miles) from southern Corfu to the smaller island of **Paxos**. Trips can be booked in most resorts. Only 2500 people live on Paxos, which measures just 10km by 4km (6 miles by 2½ miles), most in the main town and port, Gáios. Apart from tourism, the island's industries are fishing and olive growing: olive oil is a good buy, being of very high quality.

Gáios is in a lovely setting, its white houses gathered around a harbour and half-hidden from the sea by a large tree-covered island in the bay. It is a lively harbour town, made busy by visiting yachts and the countless day-trippers from Corfu and the mainland resorts, but it is still very much a working waterfront town, typical of hundreds throughout Greece. Fish tavernas are plentiful, and good beaches only a short walk away. There is only one hotel, but plenty of rooms to rent in Gáios.

Antipaxos is smaller still, making Paxos look cosmopolitan, and there is no accommodation unless you

FERRY CONFUSING

The Ionian Islands are linked by a complicated ferry network. Timetables change annually, so get a current timetable from the NTOG. One thing to note is that many tourist offices act as agents for only one of the several ferry lines. If you wish to travel on, say, a Tuesday, when a rival company operates, the office will deny the existence of that ferry and try to persuade you to book on their own next available service. Try several agencies, or contact the port authorities.

Opposite: *Antipaxos is still unspoilt and only a short boat ride from Corfu.*

PAXOS FESTIVALS

The most important date in the year is 29 June, the feast of St Peter and St Paul, when a procession takes place in the saints' honour. It visits their church, as well as the Church of the Holy Apostles and the tomb of St Gaius, who gave his name to the island's capital, Gáios. He has his own feast day on 5 November. On the tiny islet of Panayia in Gáios harbour, 15 August is an important day, with a daytime pilgrimage to the monastery there. In the evening the feast continues in the main square on Gáios with visitors not just welcomed but encouraged.

can rent a room in someone's house. Only 120 people inhabit the island all year round, living mostly off their vineyards, fruit and fishing. Boats cross regularly from Gáios, and will drop visitors at one or another of the island's numerous beautiful sandy beaches, many of which have tavernas open in season.

THE OTHER IONIAN ISLANDS

The other four main islands in the Ionian group – Lefkas, Ithaca, Cephalonia and Zákinthos – lie close together,

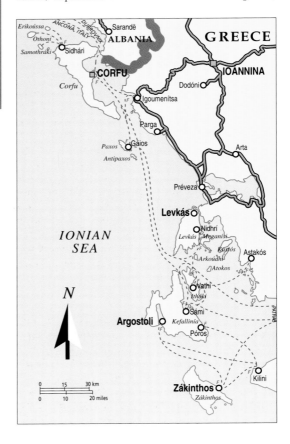

with Corfu about 60km (37 miles) to the north. Because of the distances involved, day trips are not feasible, but connections are quite good if you are prepared to stay for a night or two. Contact one of the tourist offices for ferry details. Services are obviously more frequent in summer, when there are also twice-weekly Olympic Airways flights from Corfu to Cephalonia and Zákinthos.

Zákinthos Town was rebuilt after an earthquake in 1953, but retains much of its charm.

Lefkas (Levkás) *

Hardly an island at all, Lefkas is connected to the Greek mainland by a causeway. It is an attractive, green place, where many women still wear traditional dress, and has been the slowest of the Ionian islands to develop for tourism, although that is now changing. The coast is proving very popular with windsurfers, in particular the small resorts of **Nidhrí and Vassiliki**, but inland there are many unspoilt rural villages, making Lefkas a great island for those who enjoy exploring off the beaten track. **Lefkas Town** has most of the accommodation on the island, but no beach. Similarly, the handful of villages with rooms to rent tend to be some distance from a beach. This is not a problem if you don't mind a walk, as there are numerous good sandy beaches around.

Cephalonia (Kefallinía) ***

Mountainous Cephalonia is larger than Corfu, and while parts of it have been given over very much to tourism, its size means that there are still quiet beach resorts, hill villages and deserted sandy coves. The fishing village of **Fiskárdo** is a rarity here in that its 18th-century Venetian houses remained intact after the devastating 1953 earthquake that destroyed almost every other community on Cephalonia (and on Zákinthos). The area around 1632m

> **LOVER'S LEAP**
>
> Lefkas can claim the original Lover's Leap, at Cape Doukata at the extreme southern tip of the island. The poet Sappho was allegedly the first to take the plunge over the 60m (200ft) white cliffs in the name of unrequited love, a practice continued in later years by lovelorn Roman youths, the gesture somewhat spoiled by the fact that they often strapped birds to themselves in the hope that they might fly.

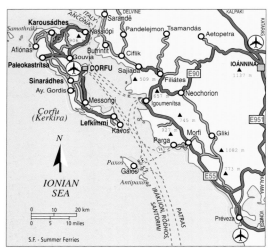

(5354ft) **Mount Énos**, the highest point in the Ionian islands, is a national park, created to protect the fir trees after which the island is named: *Abies cephalonica*. Also protected are the loggerhead turtles who have one of their main nesting sites here. There are plenty of hotels on the island.

Ithaca (Itháki) ★★

Renowned as the home island of Odysseus, rocky Ithaca has little tourism other than the day visitors who come for a change of scene or to be taken round the sites associated with Homer's hero. Not that there is any historical proof of their authenticity, but the stories *could* be true – and local guides will convince you that they are. The port and main village, **Váthi**, has a few small hotels and rooms to rent, but the island lacks good beaches.

Zákinthos ★★★

This island could hardly be more different from Ithaca. It has dozens of sweeping sandy beaches and sees a tourist invasion every summer, although the island is large enough to appeal equally to those who like to get away from the crowds. Most visitors flock to the beach resorts around **Laganás** in the south, a bay that runs for 14km (9 miles). Unfortunately this is a traditional nesting site for loggerhead turtles, and efforts are being made to preserve at least a part of the beach for their use before it is too late. Elsewhere are smaller resorts such as **Alykés** in the north, a string of mountain villages and – a popular attraction – the **Kianoú Caves** (or Blue Grotto) on Zákinthos' northern tip. Here the waters seemingly turn bathers blue; a boat trip into the Grotto is delightful.

TO THE GREEK MAINLAND

Just a short boat journey away from Corfu is the coast of Epirus, with two main destinations: Parga and Igoumenítsa.

Parga **

This is a busy and appealing seaside resort, much like many on Corfu though it has the additional charm of picturesque back streets with white houses covered in tumbling bougainvillaea and bright hibiscus. The beach is first class, with others nearby, and a day trip that allows time to visit the castle and dine at the seafront tavernas is an attractive outing from Corfu.

Igoumenítsa *

By contrast with Parga, this is a dull seaport, whose only attraction to most people will be as a means of getting to the other Ionian islands, or out into Epirus to explore the nearby mainland for a day or two.

Ioánnina ***

Ioánnina, about 50km (30 miles) from Igoumenítsa, is the capital of the Epirus region. It is a busy town but with much to offer the visitor. Here Ali Pasha (see box page 18) had his court, and his impressive castle can be visited. Ioánnina stands on a lake, in the middle of which is Nissí (meaning 'island') where, in the Monastery of Pendelímonos, Ali Pasha was killed in 1822. The bullet holes in the floorboards can still be seen.

On the edge of Ioánnina are the **Pérama Caves**, the largest cave network in Greece, with guided tours throughout the year and well worth seeing. Not to be missed is a visit to the historical site of **Dodona**, 22km (14 miles) away at the end of a winding road into the hills. The theatre here is almost 2300 years old, but the site is even older and better known as the place where the Oracle of Zeus could be consulted.

> **DOLPHINS IN DANGER**
>
> The sight of dolphins in the seas off Corfu is not uncommon. They are most easily seen when the surface is calm, making them more visible when they break the surface. The ease with which they can be spotted belies the true picture, which is that their numbers are being reduced for various reasons. One is pollution, another the fact that they are often trapped in fishing nets. The visitor can only try to avoid adding to the pollution, and express concern for their welfare to local people if the opportunity arises.

On the coast of Epirus, opposite Corfu, Parga is the most attractive of several resorts in the area.

There are no ancient theatres on Corfu, but this one at Dodona near Ioánnina is one of the best in the whole of Greece.

Albania ★★★

At the time of writing, boat trips to nearby Albania have been suspended by the Greek government due to political disputes between the two countries. The trips may well be resumed in the future, however, so you are advised to check when you are in Corfu. When the situation allows it, an hour-long crossing takes you from Corfu Town to Sarande. The trip is even shorter if taken from one of the northeastern Corfu resorts. From Sarande an optional excursion is usually available to the Roman remains at **Butrinti**, and meals can be taken in traditional restaurants with folk dancing displays. Two-day tours require advance notice and the purchase of a visa for an overnight stay.

FURTHER AFIELD

From Ioánnina you could head north to the Pindus Mountains and the **Vikos Gorge**, the second-longest gorge in Europe after Crete's Samaria Gorge, but much more rugged and remote. The gorge is surrounded by the fascinating **Zagorian villages** (see box). East of Ioánnina is the traditional mountain village of Métsovo, and beyond that the unique hilltop monasteries of the **Meteora** perched atop the weird rock formations which jut out of the Plain of Thessaly. Further east still is the home of the Gods, **Mount Olympus**. South from Ioánnina spectacular roads lead through the hills of northern Greece to the Gulf of Corinth and the **Peloponnese**.

ZAGORIAN VILLAGES

The Zagorian villages – 46 of them – that cluster round the Vikos Gorge north of Ioánnina have a very distinctive look. Narrow cobbled lanes meander between stone houses, many of them formerly grand mansions built with money remitted by Zagorian men forced to seek work away from their poor and remote homeland. The villages are linked by ancient footpaths, taken across rivers by sturdy packhorse bridges. Some of the villages are now crumbling, others are inhabited by just a few families, while the more accessible flourish, many boasting one small hotel and basic tourist facilities.

Excursions at a Glance

BEST TIMES TO VISIT

There can be pressure on accommodation in July and August, and no accommodation to be had in out-of-the-way places from November to Easter, so **May–June** and **September–October** are ideal, both practically and for the weather.

GETTING THERE

There are hourly **ferries** between Corfu Town and Igoumenítsa, and several ferries a week that go from Corfu Town to Paxos, Ithaca, Cephalonia and on to Patras in the Peloponnese. In season these are augmented by other services, such as hydrofoils between Corfu Town, Lefkas, Ithaca, Paxos, Cephalonia and Préveza on the mainland. In addition there are day trips to Parga, Paxos and Antipaxos. The other Ionian islands are mostly linked to one another by direct ferries, which also connect with the mainland.

GETTING AROUND

Car hire is available in all the ports listed, except for Ithaca, Paxos and Antipaxos, where cars are irrelevant. In midsummer it would be advisable to book ahead through the nearest tourist office. Bicycles, mopeds and motorcycles can be hired on Lefkas, Cephalonia and Zákinthos. The larger islands have good **bus** services, as do the mainland ports, both local and long-distance, linking them with Athens.

WHERE TO STAY

Cephalonia
Xenia: the only B class hotel in Argostoli, the main town; expensive but good, tel 0671-22233.
Igoumenítsa
Epirus: C class hotel, near to the port, clean and not too expensive, tel 0665-22504.
Ioánnina
Olympic : C class, central and comfortable, tel 0651-25888.
Ithaca
Hotel Mentor: B class hotel on Váthi quayside, best of a limited choice, tel 0674-32433, fax 0674-32293.
Lefkas
Hotel Xenia: a pleasant old-established B class hotel in Lefkas Town, tel 0645-24762.
Parga
Paradissos: although only 'D' class this has excellent facilities, tel: 0684-31229.
Paxos
Paxos Beach: in Gáios, the only decent hotel on the island (B class), but requires half-board accommodation, tel 0662-31211.
Zagorian Villages
EOT Guesthouse: restored traditional house in Megalo Papingo, tel 0653-41615.
Zákinthos
Strada Marina: convenient large B class hotel near the port, tel 0695-22761.

WHERE TO EAT

Cephalonia
Perivolaki, in Argostoli: wonderful, small, family-run restaurant serving authentic

island dishes, tel 0671-22779.
Ioánnina
Taverna Propodes, on Nissí island: a delightful place for an evening meal.
Ithaca
To Trehandiri, in the market area of Váthi: authentic tasty Greek food, tel 0674-33066.
Lefkas
Regantos, on the main square of Lefkas Town: traditional old taverna serving local specialities.
Parga
To Stelio: good seafood restaurant on the seafront.
Paxos
Taka Taka, in Gáios: delightful garden restaurant, good fresh fish, tel 0662-31323.
Zákinthos
Mantalena, near Alykés: some of the island's best home-cooked food.

TOURS AND EXCURSIONS

Excursions can be booked at any number of tourist offices, and you are unlikely to find any variation in price by shopping around, though you may find some offices offering a wider choice of options.

Corfu Town
Most trips to Albania were run by the **Petrakis Shipping Company**. If services resume, book direct at their offices at El. Venizelou 9 (tel 0661-31649/38690/34345). Particularly helpful is **Airtour Greece**, which is also the office for Olympic Airways at Kapodistriou 24 (tel 0661-33182/39466).

Travel Tips

Tourist Information

The Greek National Tourist Organization (NTOG) has its office in Corfu Town at the corner of Zavitsianou and Velissariou, which is where the entrance is although the address is Platia Elevtherias 1, Corfu Town, 49100 Corfu, Greece, tel 0661-37638. There is another smaller office about 50 metres away in New Fortress Square, tel 0661-37520. Practical advice is also available from the Tourist Police in the west wing of the Palace of St Michael and St George, tel 0661-30265.

Municipality of Corfu Tourist Information Offices are situated at the New Port, tel 0661-28509, with information kiosks on the Esplanade and San Rocco Square. There are private 'Tourist Offices' in every resort, and these sell boat tickets, rent out cars, and offer excursions and other services. Most will happily give general advice without charge.

There are also NTOG offices in:

Australia
51–7 Pitt Street, Sydney, NSW 2000, tel (02) 241-1663, fax (02) 235-2174

Canada
1300 Bay Street, Main Level, Toronto, Ontario M5R 3K8, tel (416) 968-2220, fax (416) 968-6533
1223 Rue de la Montagne, Montreal, Quebec H3G 1Z2, tel (514) 871-1535, fax (514) 871-1498

UK
4 Conduit Street, London W1R 0DJ, tel (0171) 734-5997, fax (0171) 287-1369

USA
645 Fifth Avenue, New York, NY 10022, tel (212) 421-5777, fax (212) 826-6940
168 North Michigan Avenue, Chicago, IL 60601, tel (312) 728-1084, fax (312) 782-1091
611 West 6th Street, Suite 1998, Los Angeles, CA 90017, tel (213) 626-6696, fax (213) 489-9744

Entry Documents

If visiting for less than three months, a passport valid for the whole period of your stay is all that is required for EU citizens and for most other countries too. Longer stays require a **visa**, so contact the Tourist Police or NTOG if this proves necessary. Some nationalities may require visas, so check if uncertain. You may be refused entry to Greece if your passport bears a stamp from northern (Turkish-occupied) Cyprus.

Customs

The amounts of wine, spirits, tobacco, cigars, cigarettes and other goods that can be taken into and out of Corfu vary enormously depending on whether you are travelling to or from an EU country, a non-EU European country or a country outside Europe, and also according to whether the goods were bought duty-free or duty-paid. Visitors should check in their country of residence before travelling.

Antiquities and works of art pre-1830 cannot be exported from Greece without permission, such permission being rare. The importation of some prescription drugs is illegal without supporting medical documentation, and codeine cannot be imported. There is no limit on the import or export of foreign currency or travellers' cheques, but amounts over the value of $1000 must be declared on arrival. Non-residents may bring in up to 100,000 drachmas and export up to 20,000 drachmas in denominations no larger than 1,000 drachma notes.

Health Requirements

No vaccination certificates are required if visiting Corfu, unless you have recently been to a country where yellow fever or cholera are prevalent.

Air Travel

Corfu has one airport, on the southern outskirts of Corfu Town. There is no public bus service, but a courtesy coach meets Olympic Airways scheduled flights and takes passengers to the airline's office in Kapodistriou (where you can also pick up a coach for your return flight). There is a taxi rank directly outside the terminal. As happens universally, journeys to and from the airport are frequently overcharged, so insist that the taxi meter is switched on. The fare from the airport to Corfu Town should not exceed 1000 drachmas. If in doubt, ask for a receipt with a note of the driver's number and take the matter up with the Tourist Police.

There are a few direct scheduled flights to Corfu from some European cities, and dozens of direct charter flights from Europe every week in summer. At other times, flights to Corfu will

require a change in Athens and a domestic flight with Olympic Airways. The flight from Athens to Corfu takes about one hour, and there is a daily service, although winter flights may be cancelled if the plane is not sufficiently full. Always reconfirm your reservation two to three days before departure.

Road Travel

Corfu has a good road network and, being a small island, can be largely covered in a few days. Take care driving on mountain roads, watching out for rough surfaces, blind bends and wandering animals. Corfu Town is best avoided, as the streets can be chaotic, some are pedestrianized, parking is difficult and a one-way system operates which can suddenly take you out of your way.

A knowledge of the Greek alphabet is helpful if travelling off the main roads, although all the major resorts have road signs in both Greek and English. Hitch-hiking is not usually a problem in Greece. Drivers stop fairly readily, and any reluctance is mainly due to the fact that most Greek motor insurance does not cover the driver for damage to passengers.

Driver's Licence:
Theoretically an International Driver's Licence is required if driving in Greece or when renting a car, but in practice only a valid driver's licence will be requested, unless yours happens to be in a particularly obscure language.

Road Rules: Greek drivers ignore most of these, so the visiting driver should be doubly cautious. This is not a facetious comment: Greece has one of the worst accident rates in Europe. Maintain a safe distance between yourself and any driver in front, and keep well in to the side when going round bends as Greeks like to drive down the middle of the road. Officially they drive on the right, and should give priority to traffic coming from the right unless otherwise indicated. Seat belts are compulsory and it is forbidden to sound your horn in built-up areas. You must also carry a warning triangle, a fire extinguisher and a first aid kit.

Speed Limits: 50kph (31mph) in built-up areas, 80kph (49mph) outside these and 100kph (62mph) on motorways and dual carriageways.

Fuel: Unleaded petrol is widely available, and petrol stations are plentiful, though they may be closed on Sundays and during the afternoon.

Car Hire: There are about 25 car rental firms in Corfu Town, including the major international names. Several of these also have offices at the airport and many have agencies in the major resorts. A reputable name may be more expensive, but the car is likely to be more regularly checked. Agreements can be for limited or unlimited mileage, so be sure you know what you are getting. Also check the **insurance cover**

carefully, as some policies do not cover damage to third parties. Be sure you have Collision Damage Waiver insurance.

Maps

Good road maps in most of the major European languages are widely available in Corfu, and almost all include a street plan of Corfu Town. If planning to drive to out-of-the-way places, it might be useful to choose a map which also shows place names in Greek.

Clothes: What to Pack

If travelling between June and September, **travel light**. Corfu is informal as well as warm, and very few places other than the casinos require formal dress. Take a sweater for the occasional cool evening, and an umbrella in the spring and autumn. Both men and women should have some means of covering up slightly if planning to visit a monastery, otherwise shorts, T-shirts and casual wear is all that is needed.

Money Matters

The Greek currency is the drachma, usually abbreviated in Greek as Δρχξ. There are coins worth 10, 20, 50 and 100 drachmas, and notes for 100, 500, 1000 and 5000. In shops, amounts are usually rounded up or down to the nearest 10 drachmas, so if you offer a 100 drachma note for a 95 drachma bill, don't expect change.
Currency Exchange: You

can change foreign currency or travellers' cheques at banks, post offices, bureaux de change and at many hotels and tourist offices. There are dozens of such places in Corfu Town, including American Express and Thomas Cook. Travellers' cheques can often be used to pay bills in hotels and some restaurants.
Banks: There are no banks outside Corfu Town, but bank buses tour the island. Opening hours are normally 08:30–14.00 from Monday to Friday only, although in season some may open in the evenings and on weekend mornings for currency exchanges. A separate window is usually used, so look for the 'Exchange' sign. You will need your passport to change travellers' cheques but not for currency.

Credit Cards: Most large shops, restaurants, car hire firms and hotels accept major international credit cards, but many smaller ones do not, so don't assume that you can survive in Corfu on plastic money only. Always have some currency or travellers'

cheques. Eurocheques are even less widely accepted, though some outlets will take them.
Sales Tax: Prices in restaurants are in two columns, without and with tax: the customer must pay the higher price. Otherwise, the price you see is the price you pay, although tourists will inevitably pay more for a drink than local customers.
Tipping: Tipping is informal throughout Greece. The usual practice in restaurants or with taxi drivers is to tell them to keep the change. Add a little if you feel you have had very good service. In tavernas, it is common to leave a tip of perhaps 100 drachmas for the young boy employed to serve wine and clear tables. In hotels, a small tip for porters and for chambermaids at the end of your stay is not expected but will be appreciated.

Accommodation

Accommodation is graded by the Tourist Police from Luxury through to E class establishments, which provides a fair guide to standards but is not

CONVERSION CHART		
FROM	**TO**	**MULTIPLY BY**
Millimetres	inches	0.0394
Metres	yards	1.0936
Metres	feet	3.281
Kilometres	miles	0.6214
Hectares	acres	2.471
Litres	pints	1.760
Kilograms	pounds	2.205
Tonnes	tons	0.984
To convert Celsius to Fahrenheit: $x \times 9 \div 5 + 32$		

infallible. Facilities such as telephones in the rooms will count for more than the fact that the room is rather dingy. Corfu has five luxury hotels, two in Corfu Town and one each in Komméno, Kondókali and Moraïtika. There are A class hotels in almost all major resorts, and both A and B class hotels generally have all or most rooms with private facilities, some with telephones and televisions. C class would normally lack private facilities, but usually be clean, whereas D and E class are very much the budget choices. Apartments are also checked by the Tourist Police.

An official notice of the grade and the room price (based on a Tourist Police inspection) should be displayed in the room – it's usually to be found on the back of the door. This can be slightly out of date, if the current year's inspection has not yet been carried out. A small variation in price can usually be safely ignored; if in doubt, check with the hotel management. Suspicion of gross overcharging should be reported to the Tourist Police. Breakfast is not usually included in the room price, leaving you the option of eating in or going to a local café.

'Rooms to rent' signs are common outside houses in resorts. These may be self-catering apartments or simply the use of a room in someone's house, sharing facilities with the family. These can be delightful or dreadful, so approach them with an open

mind. The signs may also read 'Zimmer' or 'Domatia'.

Plumbing

Greek plumbing uses small-bore pipes, which easily become blocked by toilet paper. Only in newer hotels will it be safe to flush paper down the toilet. Elsewhere, bins are provided in bathrooms for the disposal of toilet paper. This may seem unhygienic, but is less unpleasant than a blocked toilet.

Trading Hours

Shops normally open Monday to Saturday from 08:00 to 13:00, then close for the afternoon, reopening at about 17:00 until 20:00. Souvenir shops and others in tourist areas may stay open later, and some may stay open in the afternoon, but supermarkets and general stores will normally close. Non-tourist shops will also usually close on a public holi-

BOOKS TO BRING

Apart from the inevitable books by Lawrence and Gerald Durrell, Henry Miller's *The Colosssus of Maroussi* contains an entertaining account of the American writer's first visit to Corfu. *A Kitchen in Corfu* by James Chatto and W L Martin is a delightful description of the island through its recipes, particularly for feast days. Edward Lear's *Selected Letters* include accounts of his visits to the Ionian Islands. Botany buffs should bring *Flowers of Greece and the Aegean* by Anthony Huxley and William Taylor.

day and on a feast day. Some close on the eve of important feasts too, and may not open on the day after, depending on how well the celebrations went.

Public Holidays

These are 1 January, 6 January, First Day of Lent (Clean Monday), 25 March, Good Friday, Easter Monday, Whit Monday, 1 May, 15 August, 28 October and 25/26 December. Half holidays, when shops close in the mornings, are on 21 May and 12 December. Easter and the days dependent on the timing of Easter are according to the Orthodox calendar and do not often coincide with Easter in the rest of Europe. Greek tourist offices can give dates, if needed. The Feast of St Spiridhon on 11 August is effectively a public holiday, and many shops will also be closed on the other days when St Spiridhon's remains are carried through Corfu Town, these being Palm Sunday, Easter Saturday and the first Sunday in November.

Measurements

Greece uses the metric system.

Telephones

International direct dialling is not usually a problem from Corfu. Many Greek homes do not, however, have a telephone so great use is made of public call boxes. Many shops and kiosks on street corners have metered phones; you simply pick up the phone, dial, and pay for the metered units at the end. Metered phones are also available in some branches of the OTE (post office).

Time

Corfu is two hours ahead of Greenwich Mean Time, one hour ahead of the rest of Western Europe, seven hours ahead of the USA's Eastern Standard Time and eight hours behind Australian New South Wales Time. Corfu changes its clocks by one hour in spring and autumn in line with all EU countries, but this may not coincide with other parts of the world, so check if travelling near these dates.

Electricity

220AC voltage is used, with European sockets using two round pins.

Water

Water is perfectly safe to drink, though many visitors buy bottled water for personal preference. This is widely available in supermarkets and in restaurants.

Medical Services

The majority of Greek **doctors** speak at least one foreign language, usually English, as do many **pharmacists**, who are also trained to treat minor ailments and to prescribe drugs. Look for the green or red cross. There is always a pharmacy open 24 hours a day and its address should be displayed in every other pharmacy in the area

(though it may only be written in Greek). Newspapers also carry notices of which pharmacists are on duty.

Most towns and larger villages have a **Medical Centre**, signposted in Greek and English and normally open on weekdays from 08:00–12:00 only. Health insurance is essential, even for EU citizens who are entitled to free treatment provided that they have obtained a form E111 before travelling to Corfu. The main **hospital** is on Polikhroniou Konstanda in Corfu Town, halfway between San Rocco Square and the Platitéra Monastery. It has a 24-hour Casualty Department (tel 0661-30562/30033 or 0661-39403 for emergencies and ambulance).

Health Hazards

There are no major health hazards on Corfu, but visitors should obviously take precautions against sunburn. Food upsets are not common, though some people may react against the heavy use of olive oil in cooking and on salads. If swimming, watch out for sea urchins in rocky areas, and occasional jellyfish.

Emergencies

Dial 100, an all-purpose emergency number, or contact the local Tourist Police.

Security

Greece is one of the safest countries in the world. It may be acceptable to overcharge tourists, but few Greeks would steal from them. In

busy tourist areas such as Corfu, though, your fellow tourists may not be as honest as the Corfiots, so don't leave valuables lying around. There is nowhere on Corfu where it is unsafe to walk, even late at night, although young women walking alone late at night may attract unwanted attentions, so always use common sense.

Language

Thank You *'sas efhari-sto'*
Goodbye *'an-di-o'*
Hello *'ya-su'*
Please *'sas paraka-lo'*
Yes *'ne'*
No *'o-hi'*
Excuse me *'si-gno-mi'*
Do you speak English?
   'mi-la-te angli-ka?'
How much is it? *'po-so ka-ni?'*
Hotel *Xenodochio*
Post Office *Tachithromio*
Police *Astinomia*
Pharmacy *Farmakio*
Doctor *Iatros*
Bank *Trápeza*
Church *Eklisia*
Hospital *Nosokomio*
Café *Kafeneion*
Bus *Leoforio*
Restaurant *Estiatório*
Airport *Aerodrómio*
Food *Fagitó*
Saint *Ayía/Áyios (Ay.)*
Street *Odós*
Square *Platia*
Market *Aghora*
Ruins *Eripia*
Castle *Kastelli*
Harbour *Limani*
Peninsula *Khersónisos*
Gulf *Kólpos (Kól)*
Boat *Karávi*
Bay *Órmos*
Beach *Paralia*